ROUGH GUIDES

T0203358

ROUGH GUIDES WALKS & TOURS

KRAKÓW

YOUR TAILOR-MADE TRIP
STARTS HERE

Tailor-made trips and unique adventures crafted by local experts

Rough Guides has been inspiring travellers with lively and thought-provoking guidebooks for more than 35 years. Now we're linking you up with selected local experts to craft your dream trip. They will put together your perfect itinerary and book it at local rates.

Don't follow the crowd – find your own path.

HOW ROUGHGUIDES.COM/TRIPS WORKS

STEP 1

Pick your dream destination, tell us what you want and submit an enquiry.

STEP 2

Fill in a short form to tell your local expert about your dream trip and preferences.

STEP 3

Our local expert will craft your tailor-made itinerary. You'll be able to tweak and refine it until you're completely satisfied.

STEP 4

Book online with ease, pack your bags and enjoy the trip! Our local expert will be on hand 24/7 while you're on the road.

BENEFITS OF PLANNING AND BOOKING AT ROUGHGUIDES.COM/TRIPS

PLAN YOUR ADVENTURE WITH LOCAL EXPERTS

Rough Guides' English-speaking local experts are hand-picked, based on their experience in the travel industry and their impeccable standards of customer service.

SAVE TIME AND GET ACCESS TO LOCAL KNOWLEDGE

When a local expert plans your trip, you save time and money when you book, even during high season. You won't be charged for using a credit card either.

MAKE TRAVEL A BREEZE: BOOK WITH PEACE OF MIND

Enjoy stress-free travel when you use Rough Guides' secure online booking platform. All bookings come with a money-back guarantee.

WHAT DO OTHER TRAVELLERS THINK ABOUT ROUGH GUIDES TRIPS?

Trip to Spain

This Spain tour company did a fantastic job to make our dream trip perfect. We gave them our travel budget, told them where we would like to go, and they did all of the planning. Our drivers and tour guides were always on time and very knowledgable. The hotel accommodations were better than we would have found on our own. Only one time did we end up in a location that we had not intended to be in. We called the 24 hour phone number, and they immediately fixed the situation.

Don A, USA ★★★★★

Trip to Morocco

Our trip was fantastic! Transportation, accommodations, guides – all were well chosen! The hotels were well situated, well appointed and had helpful, friendly staff. All of the guides we had were very knowledgeable, patient, and flexible with our varied interests in the different sites. We particularly enjoyed the side trip to Tangier! Well done! The itinerary you arranged for us allowed maximum coverage of the country with time in each city for seeing the important places.

Sharon, USA ★★★★★

PLAN AND BOOK YOUR TRIP AT ROUGHGUIDES.COM/TRIPS

BAR
SZARA

KAWA
HERBATA
DRINKI

CONTENTS

Introduction

Trip plans

Directory

Catholic visitors

Visit John Paul II's student digs (walk 7), the site of his first Mass as a newly qualified priest (tour 3), and go to Mass yourself at St Mary's Basilica (walk 1).

Best walks & tours for...

Romantic types

Moonlit walks around the Planty (walk 11) are what romance is all about, while a kiss by Sigismund's Bell (tour 3) is said to guarantee eternal love.

Gourmands

Main Market Square (walk 1), with its rich variety of restaurants and cafés, is a foodie's dream, while a string of delicatessens on ul. Floriańska stocks a wide range of tasty Polish treats to take home.

Jewish Kraków

Kazimierz (tour 4) was for centuries Kraków's Jewish heart; the Old Synagogue remains a symbol of the city. Don't forgo the poignant former ghetto around Plac Bohaterów Getta (walk 12), or Auschwitz (tour 15).

Night owls

Main Market Square (walk 1) is surrounded on all sides by cafés and bars that stay open late; Kazimierz (tour 4) is considered the real home of Kraków nightlife by those in the know, however.

Big spenders

Take dinner at *Wierzynek* (walk 1), the city's most expensive and exquisite restaurant, before striking out on a spending spree in the boutiques of ul. Grodzka (walk 7).

Shopping

The little stores of Wawel Hill (tour 3) and the Cloth Hall in Main Market Square (walk 1) offer fine local wares, while the huge Galeria Krakowska (walk 11) has all your favourite international brands.

Something different

Make a beeline for the Socialist Realist enclave of Nowa Huta (walk 13), or Poland's oldest salt mine at Wieliczka (tour 16).

INTRODUCTION

An introduction to Kraków and what makes it special, what not to miss and what to do when you're there.

Discover Kraków

A city where religion and culture have long had the upper hand over trade and commerce, Kraków is in many ways Poland's soul. Respect for the past keeps it anchored firmly in tradition, while its thousands of students keep it young.

A royal capital, a university city, a centre of Catholic learning and a key focus of Jewish culture, Kraków is a city of many layers. At its heart is the only medieval town centre of Poland's major cities to survive the destruction of World War II, yet Kraków is nevertheless a forward-thinking and outward-looking city. A UNESCO World Heritage Site, it receives nearly thirteen million visitors each year – at times it can feel as if they're all clustered on the Main Market Square, although in reality the city is large enough to contain everyone, with plenty of green space affording relief, particularly in the height of summer.

With excellent road and rail links, Kraków is as good a base as any to explore the rest of southern Poland, and a number of places are accessible on easy day-trips: the mountain resort of Zakopane, the former Nazi concentration camp at Auschwitz, the Wieliczka Salt Mine and the Socialist-Realist 'new town' of Nowa Huta. Slightly further afield are no fewer than six national parks, the industrial city of Katowice and Kraków's former rival, Tarnów, which has its own charm.

Former capital of Poland

The name Kraków comes from Prince Krak, or Grakh, ruler of the Lechici, a Western Slavic people who inhabited the Lesser Poland (Małopolska) region towards the end of the seventh century, and who is credited in popular legend as the founder of the city. It is, however, generally believed Kraków was founded in about AD 950 by merchants using it as a staging post on the Amber Road from the Baltic to the Adriatic. Amber, most European of gemstones, remains a must-buy souvenir on any trip to the city, yet while the stone has been crucial to the city's development, it was the more prosaic commodity salt (mined at nearby Wieliczka since the early eleventh century) that first made Kraków rich.

Royal approval arrived a century or so later, in 1038, when Wawel Hill and its cathedral became the official residence of Polish kings. Kazimierz the Restorer moved the capital here from Gniezno shortly after. It would remain the seat of power in Poland – and the region – until the sixteenth century, and though since

Wawel Castle in deepest winter

then Warsaw has claimed political primacy, Kraków remains the cultural and religious heart of Poland.

Cultural, religious hub

The country's oldest university is in Kraków – the Jagiellonian University, founded in 1364. In 1533 the Dominicans staged Poland's first play here, and about two and a half centuries later the country's first permanent theatre, the Stary, was built. In the late nineteenth century, the Stary, and Kraków, were major players in the development of the Młoda Polska (Young Poland) movement of artists, architects, poets and dramatists, whose adaption of Art Nouveau, or Secession, styles became synonymous with the city. More recently, Kraków was one of the European Capitals of Culture chosen for the 2000 millennium.

As the city from which Karol Wojtyła (born in 1920 in Wadowice, 40km/25 miles southwest of Kraków) became Pope John Paul II in 1978, Kraków has since become a centre of Roman Catholic pilgrimage as important – to many Poles at least – as the Vatican itself. Kraków was until World War II a major centre of Jewish life and remains an important place of remembrance: the wartime ghetto the Nazis established was one of Europe's largest. Many of its inhabitants were murdered in Nazi roundups or sent to Auschwitz-Birkenau, the notorious death camp located not far to the west.

Young Poland

Young Poland (Młoda Polska) was an influential movement in art, architecture and literature which swept through Poland in the years before World War I. Partly inspired by Parisian Art Nouveau, the Viennese Secession and Germany's Jugendstil movement, it was a rebellion against the realist styles that that dominated the art of the nineteenth century. It also took inspiration from traditional Polish culture, blending folk motifs and rural architecture with modern design. One of the aims of Young Poland was to reinvigorate Polish culture at a time when the country was split between Russian, German and Habsburg empires. Undisputed capital of Young Poland was Kraków, where outstanding examples of the era's painting, architecture, stained glass and interior design can be found.

A river-threaded city

Kraków sits more than 200m (700ft) above sea level at the foot of the Carpathian Mountains, and the larger city is split in two by the Wisła (Vistula), though the areas that tourists visit are neatly encircled by the river. A city of extreme weather, Kraków can be covered in snow for two or three months of the year (December to February), yet in

Icons for sale

The wonderfully preserved Main Market Square

July and August temperatures often climb to over 30°C (86°F). Dress and plan your activities accordingly, and note that downpours are a frequent menace, even on the warmest days.

Home to some 763,000 people, Kraków is Poland's second-largest city. Nowadays, almost all of its inhabitants are Poles. Until 1941 and the Holocaust, the Jews were a significant ethnic group, making up a quarter of the city's population. Although Jewish culture in the city has undergone something of an upsurge in recent decades, fewer than a thousand call the city permanent home.

Sublime centrepiece

For a city born of trade, it is only fitting that the centre of Kraków is the sublime Main Market Square (Rynek Główny). Its centrepiece, the Cloth Hall, is for many as much a symbol of Kraków and its past as Wawel Cathedral. Once a hub for international textile trade, it now houses stalls selling a variety of wares. For most, it is the first stop on explorations of the Old Town, a fascinating grid of narrow streets. On the edge of the Main Market Square is the thirteenth-century St Mary's (Kościół Mariacki), Kraków's main civic church and a high Gothic reminder of the city's past. The prominence given to a statue of national poet Adam Mickiewicz is a sign of Kraków's links with Polish literature.

The Planty

As in many of Central Europe's historic cities, a green belt, the Planty, surrounds the Old Town and provides respite and definition. It was laid out at the beginning of the nineteenth century to replace the by then redundant city walls, Kraków having long since expanded in all directions. The park is itself ringed by major boulevards, beyond which the more modern parts of the city have their own attractions, not least Secession-era architecture.

Beyond the Old Town

There is much more to Kraków than the Old Town. Towering above all is Wawel Hill, where you will find an imposing castle and cathedral, adorned with some of Europe's finest artworks since medieval times. At its base is the district of Okół, likely the site of the first Kraków settlement. For a different side to the city, visit the ancient Jewish quarter of Kazimierz, outside the city walls and with its own distinctive character. Now experiencing a renaissance, it is the city's liveliest nightlife district and a popular haunt of students and bohemians, who throng its many bars and cafés.

West of the Old Town is Piasek, where fine old apartment buildings surround quiet, hidden courtyards. Rich Cracovians made their homes in Nowy Świat (New Town) in the nineteenth century when the Old Town became too crowded.

Cracovian elder

Across the river is Podgórze, site of the Jewish wartime ghetto, made famous by the film *Schindler's List*.

After-hours scene

Enormously popular with young visitors, and home for much of the year to a large student population, Kraków over the past decade has become famous for its nightlife. Its clubs and bars buzz with activity from dusk to dawn most nights of the week, though Kraków does not lack other kinds of entertainment. Cabaret, theatre, opera and music venues are dotted throughout the city.

Fairs and festivals

Throughout the year colourful fairs are held on Kraków's streets, none more so than the blessing of palms on Palm Sunday. On Easter Monday, the Emmaus Fair in Zwierzyniec Park brings a colourful end to the Holy Week, while Corpus Christi is marked with a parade from Wawel to Main Market Square, and followed by the popular Lajkonik parade from Salwator the Thursday after. In December, stalls selling local treats and gifts fill the Main Market Square. There are many other more modern festivals dedicated to all sorts of things, from sea shanties, to soup, to dachshunds.

Dining out

Kraków has a deserved reputation as a great place to eat out. While Polish cuisine itself is not generally regarded as being particularly sophisticated, Kraków has benefited from the influences of the Habsburg Empire, with Viennese and Hungarian specialities finding their way onto the city's menus, frequently in the form of tasty local versions. Look out for game dishes such as *kaczka* (duck) and *dzik* (wild boar). Most waiting staff in Kraków speak fairly good English, and usually a smattering of German, too; many are students subsidising their studies. Menus can usually be found in English (of a sort), and staff never seem to mind helping out.

The city's future

Kraków is looking forward to the next decade with confidence, boosted by an overhaul of the transport system. The airport continues to be the subject of huge investment, with new carriers and routes being introduced. A train station has also opened at Kraków airport to connect to the city.

Plenty has been going on in central Kraków, too. Roads and rail are being improved, with the expansion of the A4 motorway and renovation of the city's main railway station, Kraków Główny. It has Poland's first underground railway interchange, with direct access to the redeveloped bus station. Further modernisation of tramlines has also been implemented. New buildings in the city include the ICE Congress Centre and a sports stadium east of the centre. The Unity Centre comprises the 102.5m/336ft Unity Tower, the highest

Lajkonik parade in full swing

John Paul II moved to Kraków in 1938

Don't leave Kraków without...

Sipping coffee in Lenin's haunt. The quintessential Secession café in Main Market Square, *Noworolski* has played host to many revolutionaries over the years. In time off from planning his revolution, Lenin could be seen taking it easy here. See page 26.

Finding the Poles' soul at Wawel. Young Poland artist Stanisław Wyspiański said of Wawel Castle and Cathedral that 'the person who enters here becomes a part of Poland'. So plunge into the heart of things and revel in this opulent royal complex. See page 38.

Tracing the story of Schindler. Explore Podgórze, Kraków's Jewish ghetto for two years during World War II, and then tour the Oskar Schindler Factory as it unfolds its harrowing tale. Visit the poignant memorial in the district's Heroes of the Ghetto Square. See page 82.

Viewing a masterpiece by Leonardo da Vinci. Why grapple with the queues to glimpse the *Mona Lisa* in Paris or *The Last Supper* in Milan when you can see a classic Leonardo da Vinci portrait in Kraków? The stunning *Lady with an Ermine* is on display at the Czartoryski Museum. See page 53.

Stepping inside beautiful St Mary's. Kraków's most famous landmark, St Mary's Basilica has an interior to take your breath away. Don't miss the remarkable altarpiece. See page 31.

Reliving the Soviet past. Gain insight into Poland's Communist years with a visit to the suburb of Nowa Huta. Amid the monumental Socialist Realist architecture is a church built by locals to resemble Noah's Ark. See page 86.

Trying the national tipple. Think vodka and think Russia, but the Poles lay equal claim to the invention of the spirit and have many different varieties to sample. The best selection can be found in the historic Jewish district of Kazimierz, home to a lively nightlife scene. See page 44.

Seeing the works of a young genius. Polymath Stanisław Wyspiański was at the heart of the Młoda Polska (Young Poland) art movement. You can check his brilliance with his stained-glass work at St Francis on walk 6 and see his paintings in the National Museum. See pages 58 and 72.

building in the city. Kraków's historic architecture is not being forgotten, with a major long-term restoration programme underway. With almost 40,000 students, Kraków's Jagiellonian University remains one of the largest and most prestigious in the country, attracting talent, technological progress and investment to a city that remains on Central Europe's cutting edge.

Oskar Schindler's former factory is now a modern museum

Top tips for visiting Kraków

Stay in Kazimierz. The city's Jewish quarter is as lively during the evening – if not more so – as it is during the day. For the full Kazimierz experience, you can stay in one of the area's hotels; a few offer a full kosher package (see page 108).

Synagogue visits. As the last functioning synagogue in Kazimierz, Remuh is strict about men covering their heads and women their arms when visiting, as is the New Jewish Cemetery. While in Kazimierz's bohemian bars anything goes fashion-wise, it makes sense to dress appropriately for church and synagogue visiting.

Snack time. Look out for stalls selling street food including *obwarzanki* (pretzel-like bread rings flavoured with rock salt or poppy seeds) and *świderki* (literally 'little drills' – sweet, brioche-style bread fingers). Also popular are *kiełbasa* (rich sausages served with sweet mustard and a slice of bread) and *zapiekanki* (a kind of Polish pizza made of sliced baguette topped with cheese, mushrooms and ketchup).

Unlicensed cabs. Top-range hotels will often attract the attention of unlicensed cab drivers, so avoid rip-offs by making sure any taxi you use is clearly marked with its rates displayed on the window. Also be aware that some of the better-class hotels use their own official taxis, which will also often charge well above and beyond the going rate. Nasty surprises can be avoided by arranging a fee beforehand, or asking reception to call a reputable company.

What to wear. Kraków is a great city to explore on foot, so comfortable walking shoes are essential. Bring warm clothes if you're visiting in winter, as the weather can be very chilly, and remember to have something waterproof (or at least an umbrella) with you in spring or autumn, as showers are quite common.

Alfresco at a price. Note that many venues operate a dual pricing policy, with higher prices (or a simple surcharge) being applied to those sitting outside. Check before ordering.

Local guides. There are hundreds of local guides touting their trade, though not all are good. Recommended are Kraków Explorers (www.krakow explorers.com) and City Walks Kraków (www.citywalkspoland.com); both of which offer a variety of free walking tours and paid specialist tours.

Kraków Tourist Card. To save time and money pick up the two- (177zł) or three-day (200zł) Tourist Card, which entitles you to free travel on city buses and trams (day and night), and free entry in up to 40 Kraków museums. The card also offers discounts at selected restaurants and shops as well as excursions. It is available at all tourist information offices and online at www.discovercracow.com.

The exquisite domes of Wawel Cathedral

Food and drink

Polish food, based on simple ingredients and distinctive flavours, is both hearty and tasty. In Kraków, local specialities are complemented by a wide range of international restaurants serving fine cuisine.

Eating out price codes

Each restaurant and café reviewed in this Guide is accompanied by a price category, based on the cost of a two-course meal (or similar) for two, including a good bottle of wine:

€€€€ = over 200zł (£40)
€€€ = 125–200zł (£25–£40)
€€ = 70–125zł (£15–£25)
€ = below 70zł (under £15)

You will not go hungry here. The city's crop of good restaurants continues to expand, and, with a number of the better hotels hiring top chefs to oversee their kitchens, you can expect good quality, though often at a price. Many Old Town restaurants are expensive, though visitors on tighter budgets will always find *pierogi* – classic Polish dumplings – in plentiful supply. Kraków is synonymous with coffee culture, and there are small independent cafés and patisseries all over the city, with few examples of the global chains ubiquitous elsewhere.

Menus are available in English and German in most Old Town restaurants, and in many more besides.

Poles love to dine alfresco, and the city's restaurants and cafés have outside tables as soon as it is warm enough.

Polish specialities

Pork, potatoes and cabbage are the country's staples, and the national dish is *bigos*, a chunky stew of pork, other meats and sausages, cabbage, potatoes and onions, spiced with herbs and served with lashings of sour cream. Though it originates in eastern Poland, where winters are long, it is found everywhere. *Pierogi* are small, semicircular ravioli-like dumplings stuffed with meat, cheese or sometimes fruit. You can pick them up from any of the numerous inexpensive *pierogi* bars. Look out, too, for *barszcz*, a delicious red beetroot soup flavoured with lemon and garlic and served hot or cold. Home-made chicken soup is another great Polish favourite.

Given that the forests and lakes to the south and east of Kraków are full of game, the local penchant for pheasant, duck (often roasted and served with apples), venison and boar is understandable. Autumn is the best time to try game dishes, which are usually served with rich sauces and plain vegetables. Polish sausages are

The Christmas Market in Main Market Square

excellent, with the heavily smoked Gruba Krakowska a local speciality.

Snacks and sweets

For snacks, look out for *precel* stalls selling hot and vaguely sweet pretzels (also known as *obwarzanki*), usually topped with salt, or *zapiekanki*, a Polish version of pizza, with the topping piled on a halved baguette. Polish desserts, such as *kremówka*, cream cakes often covered in honey, are very sweet.

International cuisine

Some of Poland's best restaurants are in Kraków, which has a range of cuisines to rival any city in Europe; from cutting-edge Modern European to Pacific Rim Fusion, new flavours are forever being created in the city's best kitchens. Catering for the large numbers of Jewish visitors, there is a good range of Jewish restaurants, centred on Kazimierz, although not all are strictly kosher. There are decent Indian and Italian haunts and some super German-owned beer halls selling sausages with lashings of sauerkraut. The choice for vegetarians is better than in many other Eastern European cities.

Drinks

Vodka is the national spirit but beer is the more popular day-to-day drink, and it's both cheap and mostly good. Local brews include Tyskie, Warka and Żywiec, and all have a clear, crisp

Vodka

Poles like to boast that they invented vodka, in the fourteenth century, though other grain-growing countries such as Lithuania, Belarus, Ukraine and Russia have equal claims. Made from water and either grain, molasses, potatoes or sugar beet, vodka was first used as a medicine, becoming a recreational drink in the sixteenth century. Perhaps the best-known brand is Wyborowa, while flavoured blends include Goldwasser, Starka and Żubrówka (Bison Grass Vodka).

and refreshing taste. Imported beers, especially Heineken, Staropramen and Stella Artois, are a hit with trendy locals, however, and Poland boasts a plethora of craft breweries turning out excellent ales. Guinness is widely available, not just in the many Irish pubs, but is relatively expensive. Poland has a burgeoning wine industry, but most wines sold in restaurants and bars are imported.

Café culture

In Kraków, coffee (and the café) is king – a legacy of the Habsburg period. Locals will visit a café on their way to work, at lunchtime and on their way home. Yet this tradition is much more than drinking coffee: the city's cafés are debating chambers, reading rooms and places of inspiration.

Pierogi, a Polish speciality

Alfresco dining in Kazimierz

Entertainment

Kraków is Poland's cultural capital and home to its liveliest nightlife. From the theatre of the Old Town to Kazimierz's trendy bars – many of which stay open 'until the last guest leaves' – there is something for everyone.

When it comes to things to do when the sun goes down in Kraków, most people find themselves spoilt for choice. From young clubbers, who can dance until dawn in one of the city's many nightspots that cater to fans of every music genre – to sophisticated city breakers forced to choose between the philharmonic and the opera, there is plenty of everything for everyone. Cinephiles and sports fans have lots of options, too. This section gives an overview of the entertainment options on offer; for more detailed listings, see page 122.

Theatre and cabaret

The Narodowy Stary Teatr (see page 122) is the oldest theatre in Poland and here you can see the country's best stage actors. Even if you are not attending a play, both the Stary and the Juliusz Słowacki Theatre (see page 122) are worth visiting to admire their sumptuous interiors.

There is also a century-long history of cabaret in Kraków that continues today. The best (and most regular) are those at the *Piwnica pod Baranami* (see page 122) basement club.

Music and opera

The city's Szymanowski Philharmonic Orchestra (named after the celebrated late nineteenth-century/early twentieth-century Polish composer and pianist) performs at the grand concert hall of the same name (see page 122), a cavernous venue that welcomes international musicians and has an often adventurous artistic policy. Kraków's opera (Opera Krakowska, see page 122) for years suffered from a lack of a permanent home, but in 2008 took possession of its own new premises.

Jazz

Jazz fans are in for a treat in Kraków; the *Jazz Club u Muniaka* (see page 122) is one of the best in Europe. Celebrated Polish and international jazz stars play every Friday and Saturday night. Look out, too, for *Harris Piano Jazz Bar* (see page 122), a jazz and blues club whose cellar always seems full.

Nightlife

It is claimed that Kraków's Old Town has more pubs per square mile than any other city in Europe, so make sure you seek out only the very best on

Setting the mood

offer. Kraków's endless charm lies in exploring its bountiful bar scene. The line between bars and cafés remains blurred, and nowhere is this truer than in the Kazimierz district, where shadowy locales, buried in nostalgia and candlelight, transform into havens of hedonism as evening progresses. Tested favourites are: the *C.K. Browar beer hall* (see page 123) for a raucous pint with locals and visitors; and trendy *Movida* (see page 123) for a more sophisticated evening sipping cocktails.

You should also head to Kazimierz for at least a couple of drinks, and try out one or two of the bars around Plac Nowy. *Le Scandale* (pl. Nowy 9) serves great cocktails, while candlelit *Alchemia* (see page 122), with a separate space for live music, is a local institution.

Clubbing

Clubbing in Kraków once meant squelching across booze-sopped floors while the foundations shook to unimaginative chart noise. The city has grown up, however, and while the lion's share of clubs can still be found in the vaulted catacombs of Kraków's cellars, adding some disco lights and a bedroom DJ is no longer enough. Divey, lager-in-a-plastic-glass student clubs are still in abundance, but so too are cutting-edge dance floors employing dress-to-impress gate policies.

Make your first stop *Bracka Cztery* (ul. Bracka 4; www.klub.krakow.

Football

Kraków, like most of Poland, is football crazy, with the local teams Wisła Kraków and Cracovia having competed with the best in the Polish league. The two home teams, which occupy impressive new stadia facing each other across the Błonie, enjoy long-standing rivalry, dubbed the 'Holy War'. Though games are well attended they are not usually sell-outs, so getting a ticket should be easy. The season runs from July to May, with a break in December and January.

pl (see page 123), as everybody else does. A little more select are *Baccarat* (see page 122), a place the city's beautiful set has made its own, and *Choice* (ul. Floriańska 15; www.choiceclub.pl), where only the best-dressed and trendiest are granted entry.

Cinema

In the centre of Kraków, Kino pod Baranami occupies a former Renaissance palace and shows a selection of art films and prize-winning features to a cinephile crowd. (see page 123). Multi-screen cinemas include the enormous Cinema City (see page 123) at the Kraków Plaza shopping centre east of the city. Films are usually shown in their original language with Polish subtitles.

Cocktail time

Kraków brims with jazz clubs

Shopping

While never hoping to rival London, Paris, or even Warsaw, as a shopping destination, Kraków offers plenty to spend your money on, with its modern shopping centres, small boutiques and specialist stores.

Nobody comes to Kraków to shop, but treasures can be found in the city. Beyond Habsburg antiques and the ubiquitous amber, you should look out for leather goods and accessories, tableware, glassware and lace.

Cloth Hall and the markets

The first stop for many visitors – shopping or not – the Cloth Hall offers a wide selection of the kind of souvenirs you will find throughout the city and prices are much the same as elsewhere. Look out for good-quality folk art, carved wooden sculptures and toys and tasteful religious art, as well as modern jewellery and amber, which has been traded here since the city began. Kraków's other markets tend to sell produce only, but are great if you want to see people going about their daily business. The largest, Hala Targowa, with a flea market on Sunday mornings, is on ul. Grzegórzecka, a short walk east of the city centre. There's a small weekend flea market in Kazimierz in Plac Nowy, while Rynek Kleparski, just north of the Old Town, is a handy market for buying cheese, sausage, bread and other picnic supplies. In December,

the Christmas Market in Rynek Główny (Main Market Square) fills the square with stalls selling handmade goods and delicious hot local snacks.

Shopping streets

The main shopping thoroughfares in the centre are ul. Floriańska, the Main Market Square and ul. Grodzka, which link up to form a 'shopping triangle'. It can be difficult to recommend specific outlets: it's not uncommon for shops to have no street number and some stores, in keeping with the Communist legacy, display only generic titles such as 'Jeweller', with no clear name.

Two big, modern shopping centres are within easy reach of the Old Town: Galeria Krakowska (www.galeria krakowska.pl), opposite the main railway station, and Galeria Kazimierz (www. galeriakazimierz.pl), on the outskirts of Kazimierz and well served by buses and trams to Rondo Grzegórzeckie.

Opening hours

Typical hours are Monday to Friday 9/10am–7pm, Saturday 9/10am–6pm (although some close at 1pm). Small shops are closed

Ul.Grodzka is a good place to head for boutiques

on Sunday. Sunday hours for big shopping centres are changing following a ban on Sunday trading.

What to buy

Clothes and jewellery
Leather goods, including handbags, gloves, coats and luggage, are all worth taking a look at. Fur hats, sheepskin coats, jackets and accessories are widely available, which may shock visitors from countries where wearing fur is a definite no-no. In Poland wearing fur is standard during the snowy winters.

Items made from amber often represent exceptionally good value, whether in the form of rings, earrings, necklaces, bracelets, cufflinks, or even bowls and jewellery boxes. You will have no trouble finding amber in Kraków: the best is in the small shops of the Old Town, such as Boruni, in the Cloth Hall and ul. Grodzka 60.

Antiques
An array of small shops sells all sorts of wonderful knick-knacks, from Soviet-era memorabilia to antique watches and clocks. While, technically, you cannot export items produced before 1945 – unless you gain prior written permission from the appropriate government department – small personal items such as medals, badges, watches and pens are usually exempt. Reputable antique shops can arrange authorisation and onward shipping, but often at

> # Baltic gold
> Amber, Poland's national gemstone, is fossilised tree resin that once seeped from deciduous and coniferous trees, solidified and, over the course of thousands of years, matured into the form we are familiar with today. This resin sometimes traps insects and flora, and amber that contains identifiable specimens of prehistoric life is considered a special rarity, and priced accordingly. The Baltic Sea washes up amber from beneath the surface of the sand, depositing it conveniently on beaches to be collected. The colour of the translucent stone ranges across a surprising spectrum, from the more common yellow and white to stones with red and green streaks and tinges. These tints aren't flaws; they add character to the stone.

a cost. If you don't know where to begin, look in reputable DESA Dzieła Sztuki i Antyki at ul. Floriańska 13 or browse in one of the most established shops in the Old Town, the upscale Salon Antyków at ul. Jagiellońska 9.

Sweets and vodka
Confectionery made at the famous Kraków Wawel sweet factory is a good buy, as is the generally excellent Polish vodka (note that price is directly related to quality).

Amber is plentiful

Chronology

With a rich but much troubled history, Kraków still bears some of the scars from battles fought over its cultural and religious landmarks. Most have fortunately, miraculously even, survived.

Early to medieval Kraków

50,000 BC First known settlement on Wawel Hill, Palaeolithic era.

9th cent. AD Wawel Hill becomes a fortified village and the seat of the Wiślan (Vistulan) Dukes.

965 The earliest written reference to Kraków, by a Spanish merchant, describes 'a major town known throughout Europe'.

1000 The bishopric of Kraków is founded following Poland's conversion to Christianity in 966.

1038 King Kazimierz Odnowiciel (Casimir the Restorer) moves the capital of Poland from Gniezno to Kraków and builds a royal residence on Wawel Hill.

1079 St Andrew's, one of Poland's earliest Romanesque churches, is founded.

12th cent. Wieliczka salt mine is established outside Kraków.

1241 Tartars destroy the town.

1257 Kraków gains municipal rights.

1290 Construction of St Mary's Basilica begins.

1335 Kazimierz is established as a separate town outside Kraków city centre.

1364 Kraków hosts an international meeting of monarchs.

1386 Grand Duke Jogaila of Lithuania marries Queen Jadwiga of Poland, becoming King Władysław II Jagiello and joining the two countries in a relationship that will last four centuries.

1400 Collegium Maius is established as the second university college in Central and Eastern Europe.

Renaissance to the Habsburgs

1499 The Barbican is completed.

1556–60 The Cloth Hall is built in Renaissance style.

1569 Poland and Lithuania form the Polish-Lithuanian Commonwealth at the Union of Lublin.

1596 King Zygmunt III Waza transfers the royal residence to Warsaw, which he declares the capital of Poland.

1665–7 Swedish invaders ravage and loot the town.

1734 King Augustus III becomes the last Polish monarch to be crowned in Wawel Cathedral.

1783 Kraków's Botanical Gardens are established.

Mythical dragon of Wawel Hill

1791 Kazimierz becomes part of Kraków.
1796 After three successive partitions of Poland, Kraków becomes part of the Habsburg Empire.
1799 Poland's longest-serving theatre, Stary Teatr, is established.
1820s The Planty gardens are laid out.
1846 Kraków leads an uprising against the Habsburg Empire.
1850 The Great Fire devastates the town's historic centre.
1879 Poland's first national museum is established in the Cloth Hall.

Twentieth century to the present

1918 Kraków becomes part of a newly independent Poland.
1939 Nazis establish administrative headquarters in the city.
1945 Red Army takes over Kraków leading to Communist, Soviet-satellite government of Poland.
1947–9 The Lenin Steelworks are built in the new suburb of Nowa Huta.
1978 Kraków's historic centre gains UNESCO World Heritage Site status; Cardinal Karol Wojtyła, Bishop of Kraków, is elected pope.
1981–3 Martial law declared in Poland.
1989 Democratic elections see free trade union Solidarity win.
2000 Kraków is declared a European City of Culture.
2004 Poland joins the European Union.

Monument to joining thr EU in 2004, Market Square

2007 The 750th anniversary of Kraków as a city.
2010 The body of Polish President Lech Kaczynski is interred at Wawel, after his death in the Smolensk plane crash.
2011 Pope John Paul II beatified; Poland takes over presidency of the EU for the first time.
2013 Kraków is officially designated UNESCO's City of Literature.
2015 The seventieth anniversary of the liberation of Auschwitz-Birkenau.
2016 Pope Francis attends World Youth Day and celebrates Mass in Kraków on the 1050th anniversary of Poland's baptism.
2018 The 100th anniversary of Poland regaining independence.
2023 The annual number of passengers handled by Kraków airport passes nine million for the first time.

World Youth Day in Kraków

TRIP PLANS

WALK 1
Main Market Square

Playing heart to Wawel's soul, the Main Market Square has been Kraków's commercial and social centre for centuries. Every building has a story and in many cases great historical importance; all visits to Kraków should start here.

DISTANCE: 1km (0.6 mile)
TIME: A half day
START: In front of St Mary's
END: St Barbara's Church
POINTS TO NOTE: The houses in Main Market Square are numbered clockwise from St Mary's (no. 4; Cloth Hall is 1–3). Try to begin this route as early in the day as possible, but note that during summer months even a 7am start will not spare you the crowds. After completing this walk at St Mary's, you can extend it by following route 2. To get an idea of the city's layout and for great panoramic views, climb to the top of the Town Hall Tower or St Mary's Watchtower.

Laid out in 1257 and measuring nearly 40,000sq m (10 acres), Kraków's **Main Market Square** (Rynek Główny) is one of Europe's largest medieval squares. It was once the scene of majestic royal parades, and official guests are still ceremoniously greeted here. On a more everyday level, the square has long been a thriving centre of commercial activity, and continues to bustle with locals and tourists.

In summer the buzz goes on late into the night. An abundance of cafés, restaurants, shops, flower stalls and street performers form a colourful, engaging atmosphere.

Burghers' houses and palaces

The imposing burghers' houses and the grand palaces surrounding the Main Market Square were once owned by the city's wealthiest merchants and aristocratic families, and a variety of facades reflect diverse architectural genres.

Begin your walk at no. 4 (the first house on the square to the left of St Mary's). The house's upper levels are in Secessionist style, redesigned at the start of the twentieth century, though the house is much older.

Cross ul. Sienna: to the left at no. 7 is the **Montelupi** or **Italian House** (Kamienica Montelupich), the site of Poland's first post office, which operated from here in the sixteenth and

Alfresco cafés line the Main Market Square

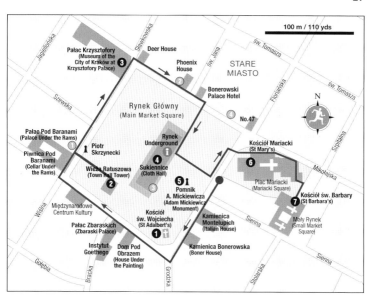

seventeenth centuries. Mail coaches would enter the rear courtyard through the narrow arch. At no. 9, **Boner House** (Kamienica Bonerowska) has retained the original ornamental attic built in the 1560s, when the house belonged to the king's private banker, Jan Boner. **L concept 13** (see page 116), on the corner of the square, is a great coffee and cake location for a little early-morning pick-me-up before moving on.

St Adalbert's

In the far southeastern corner of the square, and set slightly below current ground level, little **St Adalbert's** **Church ❶** (Kościół św. Wojciecha) dates back to the early twelfth century. This tiny Romanesque church, resembling an elegant white cube with a Gothic cupola, has room for only a few pews.

Nevertheless, its impressive interior features frescoes combining restraint and detailed ornamentation, including one of St Adalbert being killed by the Prussians after trying to convert them in AD 997.

The vaults

The vaults of St Adalbert's house a small exhibition on the history of

House under the Painting

the square. Here, visitors can see Romanesque and pre-Romanesque fragments of an even larger stone church, the remnants of a wooden church believed to be the first in Kraków, and the wooden remains of an even earlier pagan temple on display.

The southern facade

The city's most historic restaurant, **Wierzynek**, behind St Adalbert's and to the right at no. 15, comprises two Renaissance houses. One of the dining rooms features original fourteenth-century Gothic arches, and the wine bar and grill is situated in a fourteenth-century cellar (see page 119). The seventeenth-century **House Under the Painting** (Dom Pod Obrazem) at no. 19 features a beautiful fresco of the Blessed Virgin Mary ascending into heaven, completed in 1718. On the ground floor, **Słodki Wentzl** (see page 119) sells Kraków's best ice cream. The **Zbaraski Palace** at no. 20, which houses the Goethe Institute, was built in the fourteenth century, though its Neoclassical facade dates from the eighteenth century, when the arcaded courtyard was added.

Following the square around to the western facade, the fourteenth-century **Pałac Pod Baranami** (Palace Under the Rams) at no. 27 was refashioned in the mid-nineteenth century. The basement is occupied by the *Cellar Under the Rams* (Piwnica Pod Baranami), a cabaret and music venue. Its founder Piotr Skrzynecki is honoured with a statue in front of the **Vis-à-Vis** bar next door, see ①.

Town Hall Tower

Opposite *Vis-à-Vis* is all that remains of the magnificent **Town Hall** (Ratusz): the **Town Hall Tower** ② (Wieża Ratuszowa; www.muzeum krakowa.pl). This handsome 70m (230ft) -high red-brick tower is inlaid with decorative stone and is principally fourteenth-century Gothic, with sixteenth-century Renaissance additions. The main town hall was demolished in 1820, at the same time as much of the city's defensive walls and towers, and it was only due to sustained protests by prominent locals that the tower was saved. It doesn't take long to view the remaining tructure (and much of that time is spent negotiating steep, narrow stairs). Beside the Town Hall Tower is a large modern sculpture of a head on its side that children like to climb; this is *Eros Bendato* by Igor Mitoraj (1944–2014), who studied at Kraków's Academy of Art.

Exhibitions

The first floor of the tower, originally a chapel, houses a collection of architectural fragments, though it is now mainly used for exhibitions. The third floor's photographic display shows how the tower looked during the nineteenth century, and the

Eros Bendato sculpture by Igor Mitoraj

top floor offers excellent views of Kraków. Visitors can also admire the old clock mechanism, which is now synchronised with the atomic clock.

Museum of the City of Kraków

Towards the northern side of the square, the seventeenth-century **Krzysztofory Palace** ❸ (Pałac Krzysztofory; Rynek Główny 35; www.muzeumkrakowa.pl) houses the Museum of the City of Kraków (Muzeum Historyczne Miasta Krakowa), with a richly detailed display delving into the daily life and customs of the city. It also hosts temporary exhibitions, including a not-to-be-missed annual display of *szopki* or Christmas cribs made by local craftspeople. The opulent Fontana Room, open to the public for concerts and other special occasions, has fine plasterwork by Baldassere Fontana from the end of the seventeenth century.

Next door at no. 34 is **Hawełka**, one of the city's most enduring restaurants, great for lunch or dinner (see page 115).

The northern facade

Though the northern facade is less impressive than the square's other frontages, the Baroque **Deer House** at no. 36, once an inn, and the classic townhouses at nos 38 and 39 are worthy of inspection. The **Phoenix House** at no. 41 is home to the excellent **Loża Klub Aktora** café, see ❷.

The *Bonerowski Palace Hotel*, (see page 106), on the corner of ul. św Jana, was once another possession of the wealthy Boner family. Later, it became the home and gallery of Feliks Jasieński (1861–1929), an influential nineteenth-century art collector.

At no. 47 is **Kamienica Margrabska** (Margrave's House), which sports a wonderful oversized entrance and was once a mint. Today, fittingly, it is a bank.

Cloth Hall

At the centre of Main Market Square is the magnificent **Cloth Hall** ❹ (Sukiennice). Originally a covered market with stalls, shops and warehouses selling cloth and textiles, a building was first erected here in the mid-thirteenth century. After the hall was almost destroyed by fire, Giovanni Maria of Padua (known as Padovano) designed the current Renaissance facade, including the loggias at either end, in 1556–60. The ornamental attic, decorated with mascarons for which Kraków's most distinguished burghers apparently posed, was the work of Santi Gucci of Florence. The roof also features copper globes surmounting small spires. During recent renovations it was discovered that these globes contained historical documents from the late eighteenth to the mid-nineteenth century – there is a long tradition of builders secreting items for posterity in such 'time capsules'.

Cloth Hall, the centrepiece of Main Market Square

In the period immediately after World War II, plans were drawn up by Poland's newly installed Communist authorities to give the square a more proletarian look by ripping down Cloth Hall and replacing it with a Modernist Town Hall. Fortunately, good sense prevailed and the Cloth Hall survived.

Ground floor

The ground floor of the Sukiennice retains its commercial role. Stalls here sell folk arts and crafts, amber and silver jewellery, leather goods and good-quality souvenirs. The arcades added in 1875–9 on either side of the building now house attractive cafés. A delightful example, at no. 1, is the Secessionist-style **Kawiarnia Noworolski**, see ③.

First-floor gallery

On the first floor, the **Sukiennice Gallery** (Galeria Sukiennice; www.mnk.pl) was Poland's first national museum, and now holds a stunning collection of nineteenth-century art. When it opened in 1879, Jan Matejko, famous for grand canvases depicting national historical themes, was among the artists who donated their own work. In addition to the works of Polish artists such as Matejko, Józef Chełmoński, Władysław Podkowiński and Pius Weloński, the collection features

foreign artists in Poland, including the Italian Marcello Bacciarelli. You will also find the Tourist Information Centre on this floor.

Rynek Underground

The Kraków we see above ground looks old enough, but this exhibition (Podziemia Rynku; www.podziemia rynku.com) traces its history back to the Celts and beyond. From the entrance on St Mary's side of the Cloth Hall, descend 4m (13ft) under the square to see artefacts excavated during the renovation of the Main Market Square, which provided evidence of eight hundred years of uninterrupted trade on this site. Interactive multimedia displays show Kraków's place at the heart of European life from the tenth to the fourteenth centuries.

Adam Mickiewicz Monument

Directly outside the Sukiennice in the Main Market Square is the **Adam Mickiewicz Monument** ⑤ (Pomnik Adama Mickiewicza), a popular meeting point for locals. It honours Poland's greatest romantic poet, Adam Mickiewicz. Designed by Teodor Rygier, it was unveiled in 1898 on the centenary of the poet's birth. Mickiewicz never actually visited Kraków, at least not during his lifetime. On the thirty-fifth anniversary of his death his body was brought here and placed in Wawel Cathedral crypt. The monument is

Veit Stoss's triptych, St Mary's

the venue for Kraków's popular pre-Christmas crib competition. On the first Thursday of December, exquisitely decorated *szopki* are brought to the square by amateur craftspeople from all over Lesser Poland.

Other traditional events held in Main Market Square include the colourful Lajkonik pageant shortly after Corpus Christi. This sees a procession of people dressed as Tartars marching through the streets led by the *Lajkonik* – according to legend, one of the Vistula River rafters disguised as a Tartar riding a hobbyhorse that dances to the beat of accompanying drums. It's considered good luck to be touched by the *Lajkonik*'s wooden mace.

St Mary's Basilica

The most important building in the Main Market Square is the imposing, twin-towered **St Mary's Basilica ❻** (Kościół Mariacki). This church has two entrances, one for tourists at the rear (charge), the other (the main entrance) for regular worshippers or for those (excluding tourists) attending Mass.

Construction of this triple-naved Gothic basilica began in 1288, incorporating some fragments of an earlier Romanesque church that was burnt during the Tartar invasion of 1221.

St Mary's was privately funded and, according to the medieval Polish chronicler Jan Długosz, it

Adam Mickiewicz

Few poets have the honour of being declared a nation's eternal poet; Adam Mickiewicz (1798–1855) is probably unique in having had the honour bestowed on him in two countries. For just as Mickiewicz is adored in his adopted Poland, so he is revered in Lithuania, where he spent much of his early life, and where he is known as Adomas Mickevičius. The fact that his most famous poem – *Pan Tadeusz*, written of course in Polish – begins with the line 'O Lithuania, My Fatherland...' only confuses things further. Mickiewicz's epic poetry delved deep into Polish historical themes, and served as a rallying cry for patriots at a time when the country languished under foreign rule. Mickiewicz himself was forced into exile in Paris, and died of cholera in Istanbul while organising a volunteer army to fight against the Russian Empire.

immediately became the city's principal parish church. The side chapels and towers were only completed in the early fourteenth century. The shorter of the two is the bell tower; the other, more ornamental tower bears a late Baroque 'crown' on the spire dedicated to the Virgin Mary, and served as a city watchtower.

Cloth Hall sculpture   City museum exhibits

The beautiful, intricate interiors, dating variously from the Gothic, Renaissance and Baroque eras, repay a leisurely visit. The late nineteenth-century polychromy was designed by leading Polish artists, including Jan Matejko and Stanisław Wyspiański, with the stained-glass windows also designed by Wyspiański and Józef Mehoffer.

Veit Stoss's masterpiece

The church's most extraordinary work of art is the late Gothic triptych altarpiece entitled *The Lives of Our Lady and Her Son Jesus Christ*. This was completed between 1477 and 1489 by the Nuremberg master carver Veit Stoss (known in Poland as Wit Stwosz), who was considered the finest craftsman of his age.

The altarpiece incorporates over two hundred carved figures (many of them based on contemporary Cracovians) and decorative elements made from linden wood. The central panel, 13m (42ft) high and 11m (36ft) wide depicts the Virgin Mary falling into an eternal sleep, surrounded by the Apostles. It is considered perhaps the finest piece of Polish sculpture ever executed. Side panels depict scenes from the life of the Virgin Mary and Jesus.

Incredibly, a shift in artistic trends during the seventeenth century saw an attempt to replace the masterpiece with a plasterwork sculpture: only the Swedish invasion of 1655 prevented its total destruction, though part – it was originally much larger – was lost for ever.

Another Stoss masterpiece, a stone cross known as the *Slacker Crucifix* and depicting Christ in some discomfort on the cross, can be seen in the south aisle. After completing the cross and altarpiece, Stoss remained in Kraków, where he worked for the king and aristocrats for a further twenty years.

The trumpeter

Every hour, on the hour, day and night, a trumpeter from the local fire brigade plays the *hejnał*, a short tune, from the taller **tower**. This tradition originates from the time a watchman, seeing the Tartars prepare to scale the city walls at dawn, blew his trumpet to raise the alarm. The Tartars fired a salvo of arrows at the watchman and after a few notes he was hit in the throat. Although the tune was cut off in mid-melody, the town was roused from sleep and defended itself.

In memory of this event, the *hejnał* is played four times on every hour (to the four sides of the world) and every time it is stopped abruptly.

St Barbara's

Behind St Mary's Basilica on **Mariacki Square** (Plac Mariacki), laid out at the beginning of the eighteenth century on the site of the former parish cemetery, is **St Barbara's Church** ❼ (Kościół

Adam Mickiewicz statue

św. Barbary). Apparently, the church was constructed with the materials left from the construction of St Mary's, and by the same craftspeople. It originated in 1338 as the cemetery chapel. The small facade features a Renaissance portal as well as fifteenth-century late Gothic sculptures depicting Christ in the Garden of Gethsemane.

Sacral art

The Baroque interiors, effectively painted in two shades of blue, also include three Gothic works of sacral art – the *pietà* sculpture, a crucifix, and polychromy depicting the Apprehending of Christ. Additional polychromy on the vaulted ceiling was completed by Piotr Franciszek Molitor in 1765. The seventeenth-century main altar has paintings of the Virgin Mary and St Barbara (who died in 1621 and is buried in the crypt), plus a finely carved altar rail.

Chapel

The seventeenth-century Chapel of the Blessed Virgin Mary features the miraculous icon of Matka Boska Jurowicka (the Madonna of Jurowice), brought to Kraków in 1885 from the town of Jurowice, where the cult of the Blessed Virgin Mary developed. Finish up your walk with a well-deserved coffee or hot chocolate at **Pijalnia Czekolady E. Wedel** on the northeastern corner of the Main Market Square at no. 46, see ④.

Food and drink

① Vis-à-Vis
Rynek Główny 29;
tel: 012 422 69 61
Another Main Market Square café that is just as popular with locals as visitors, and as such is a great place to people-spot. €€

② Loża Klub Aktora
Rynek Główny 41; www.loza.pl
One of the newer breed of multi-purpose Kraków cafés, this place does a good range of sandwiches and cakes in the day, becoming a trendy drinking venue at night. €€€

③ Kawiarnia Noworolski
Rynek Główny 1/3; tel: 515 100 998
Lenin allegedly drank coffee here, as did many of the literary types who so often made Kraków their home. No longer a revolutionary haunt, it survives as a refined monument to Kraków's belle époque. €€€

④ Pijalnia Czekolady E. Wedel
Rynek Główny 46; tel: 668 498 328
Traditional Polish café with gourmet coffee, a sumptuous array of cakes and an extensive menu of drinking chocolates. Boxes of chocolates to take away make excellent presents. €€

Stained-glass windows in St Mary's   St Barbara's ceiling

WALK 2
Skirting the Royal Route

In order to avoid the pageant-filled processions that would stretch through the Old Town whenever Poland's king returned to the city, medieval Cracovians would be forced to make lengthy detours. Starting at Small Market Square this route, packed with little gems and some of the best art and architecture in the city, follows one such detour back to Main Market Square.

DISTANCE: 1km (0.6 miles)
TIME: A half day
START: Small Market Square
END: Main Market Square
POINTS TO NOTE: Small Market Square is directly behind St Barbara's Church, which can be seen from Main Market Square. Entrance to the Czartoryski Museum is restricted to a specific time slot, best booked in advance.

Small Market Square

The start of our walk, the **Small Market Square ❶** (Mały Rynek), served as the city's meat market until the nineteenth century. Today it hosts some good cafés for a pre-walk primer, including **Albo Tak Café** at no. 4, see ①.

Turn left at the square's northern end, on to Mikołajska, and you will see the **Kamienica Hipolitów** (Plac Mariacki 3; www.muzeumkrakowa.

pl), a seventeenth-century building sheltering re-creations of interiors of burghers' houses from the sixteenth to the twentieth centuries. Much of the fine furniture on display is original.

St Thomas the Apostle and the Holy Cross

Exiting the Kamienica Hipolitów and taking a left, head one hundred metres/yards north along ul. Szpitalna, where you'll come across the **Church of St Thomas the Apostle ❷** (Kościół św. Tomasza Apostoła) at no. 12. This is a prime example of seventeenth-century Baroque architecture.

Continuing along ul. Szpitalna, you'll reach Plac św. Ducha (Square of the Holy Spirit). On the right-hand corner of the square is the medieval Dom Pod Krzyżem, home to an institute devoted to the city's cultural heritage, but the square's real masterpiece is the Gothic **Holy Cross Church ❸** (Kościół św. Krzyża; ul. św. Krzyża 23) at the rear. The church's

Small Market Square

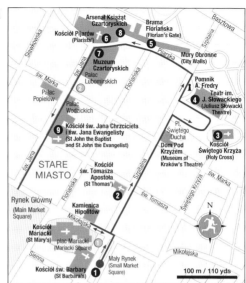

inner portal, the chapel of St Mary Magdalene and the baptismal font are fine examples of Gothic design. A chapel dedicated to the founder of the church, St Dominic, is one of the best examples of Polish Renaissance art. The impressive vaulted ceiling, supported by a single pillar, includes sixteenth-century polychromy with nineteenth-century additions by Stanisław Wyspiański. The Holy Cross Church is also known as the Actors' Church, and you can see an epitaph to the nineteenth-century Polish actress Helena Modrzejewska at the entrance.

Juliusz Słowacki Theatre

Opposite is the **Juliusz Słowacki Theatre** ❹ (Teatr im. J. Słowacki; Plac św. Ducha 1; www.teatrw krakowie.pl). One of the city's leading theatrical venues, this fabulously eclectic, neo-Renaissance gem was designed by Jan Zawiejski, who modelled it on the Paris Opéra. Built in 1893 on the site of a hospital, it features ornate interiors, including impressive stage curtains painted with allegories of comedy and tragedy.

Florian's Gate

Leave the square and push north along ul. Szpitalna. Turn left into ul. Pijarska towards **Florian's Gate** ❺ (Brama Floriańska). Once the main route to the north of the city, this is the only remaining gateway in the walls of the town's defences, which once included eight gates and almost forty bastions.

The passageway within the gate features a small, mid-nineteenth century altar with a Gothic painting of Our Lady Mary of Piaski. Part of the old city wall, together with four fourteenth-century bastions, extends on either side of Florian's

Florian's Gate   Juliusz Słowacki Theatre

Gate. This wall now serves as open-air exhibition space for local painters.

Piarists' Church

At the junction of ul. Pijarska and ul. św. Jana is the **Piarists' Church** ❻ (Kościół Pijarów), one of the city's smallest and most fascinating churches. The Piarist Order first built a chapel and adjoining residence in Kraków in 1682, after the brothers had been asked to teach students of theology at the Jagiellonian University. The congregation soon outgrew the chapel, so Duke Hieronim Lubomirski acquired a neighbouring disued brewery. Wealthy Cracovians contributed to the building costs, and the new church was consecrated in 1728.

The interiors feature Eckstein and Hoffman's illusionist murals, modelled on those of St Ignatius' Church in Rome, while the vaulted ceiling and a depiction of Christ Ascending into Heaven (copied from Raphael) by the altar are particularly impressive. Every year during Holy Week, a reproduction of Christ's Tomb is set up in the crypt of the Piarists' Church. The crypt is also sometimes a venue for exhibitions and theatre performances.

For a snack, pop into **Przypiecek** (see page 115), at ul. Sławkowska 32

Czartoryski Museum

Opposite the Piarists' Church is one of the city's most important museums,

Czartoryski Museum ❼ (Muzeum Czartoryskich; ul. św Jana 19; www. mnk.pl; note that tickets come with a specific time slot). Both this historic palace and the neighbouring monastery were acquired by the Czartoryski family in 1876 to display their magnificent art collection. The municipality donated the adjoining Renaissance Arsenal to provide further galleries. Together, these buildings offer a period setting for a fine collection that includes thirteenth- to sixteenth-century Polish, German, Italian, Spanish, Flemish and Dutch masters, sculpture, sacral art and objets d'art, as well as ancient Roman, Greek and Egyptian art. An unusual feature is the collection of Turkish tents, suits of armour and other military effects acquired at the Battle of Vienna in 1683, when King Jan III Sobieski led the victorious charge against the Ottoman aggressors. The Polish haul included Turkish coffee cups – the first coffee drunk in Poland was taken from the Turkish pavilions.

In 2016, the Polish State Treasury purchased the entire Czartoryski collection, including the buildings, from the Czartoryski family and the museum is now part of the National Museum in Kraków. As well as an extensive collection of Greek and Roman statuary, the museum's standout attraction is the *Lady with an Ermine*, painted by Leonardo da Vinci in around 1490. Thought to represent Cecilia Gallerani, mistress of Duke

The passageway within Florian's Gate

Ludovico Sforza of Milan, it is one of Leonardo's most touching portraits, and arguably packs more charisma than his much-feted *Mona Lisa*.

The Arsenal

Across the street from the Czartoryski Museum is the **Arsenal ❽** (ul. Pijarska 8; www.mnk.pl), a chunky Italianate building used to house part of the Czartoryski collection (and entered from the Czartoryski Museum via a Venetian-style bridge). The other half of the building contains a separate collection of armour through the ages.

Just along from the museum is the **Farina**, a good choice for a long lunch, see ❷.

Church of the Sts John

Head south along ul. św. Jana. On the left, just before ul. św. Tomasza, is the **Church of St John the Baptist and St John the Evangelist ❾** (Kościół św. Jana Chrzciciela i św. Jana Ewangelisty). While the foundations and crypt of the original twelfth-century Romanesque church have survived, the predominantly Baroque characteristics derive from the seventeenth century.

Adjacent to the main altar is a painting of *Matka Boża od Wykupu Niewolników* (*Holy Mary Mother of God, of Releasing Prisoners of War*) also known as *Matka Boska Wolności* (*Holy Mary Mother of God of Liberty*), which was donated by the Lithuanian Duke Stanisław Radziwiłł – who

---

Food and drink

❶ Albo Tak Café
Mały Rynek 4
A young crowd of locals, expats and visitors has made this little place the best location on Small Market Square. The prices help – it is one of the cheapest haunts in the Old Town – as does the quirky decor and friendly staff. A good place for a coffee or beer; little food served though. €

❷ Farina
Ul. św. Marka 16
Housed in a lovely historic house, *Farina* specialises in (mostly Mediterranean) fish and seafood but also serves an excellent selection of pasta and *pierogi*. Many of the dishes are traditional in inspiration but come with a modern, creative twist. €€€

---

acquired it in Spain – in about 1577. Since the early seventeenth century, this painting has been associated with those Polish prisoners of war who were 'miraculously' freed after being sentenced to death by the Ottomans. The handcuffs of one such liberated prisoner still hang by the painting. King Jan III Sobieski, who, after defeating the Turks at the Battle of Vienna, prayed here in 1684 as a token of gratitude.

Continue along ul. św. Jana to return to Main Market Square.

Piarists' Church ceiling

Czartoryski Museum

TOUR 3
Wawel

Before there was Kraków, there was Wawel, and this route takes in both the royal castle and the cathedral, including the sumptuously furnished apartments that were once home to Poland's kings. Arrive early – to see everything, you are best advised to spend a whole day here.

DISTANCE: N/A – the tour is spent in the grounds of Wawel

TIME: A full day

START: Wawel Castle

END: Dragon's Cave

POINTS TO NOTE: Access Wawel via a route leading from Podzamcze to Herbowa Gate; the ticket office is to your right on the square. Or enter via Bernadyńska Gate, at the top of the path opposite the end of ul. Grodzka: a visitors' centre is on the left. Buy cathedral tickets at the office opposite the cathedral entrance. Visitor numbers on the hill are restricted and entry to some sights is by timed ticket only. The ticket offices close 75min before the exhibitions; to reserve tel: 012 422 51 55 ext. 219. Collect reserved tickets at the office near the entrance to the arcaded courtyard at least 20min before the reserved time. Visit www.wawel.krakow.pl for more information.

Wawel Castle and Cathedral are poised proudly on a 228m (750ft) -high limestone hill overlooking the Wisła (Vistula) River. For food options while you're here, *Kawiarnia pod Basztą* next to the visitors' centre offers hot meals, snacks and drinks, and has two café terraces for fine days. *Słodki Wawel Café* sells drinks and ice creams. Both are reasonably priced but can get crowded. You could also bring a packed lunch to eat in the gardens or try one of the huddle of restaurants further down the hill, such as **Art Restauracja** on ul. Kanonicza, see ❶.

Background

Wawel Hill was established as the royal residence in 1038 when King Kazimierz Odnowiciel (Casimir the Restorer) transplanted the capital from Gniezno to Kraków and began building a royal home here. Under King Kazimierz Wielki (Casimir the Great, 1333–70) this residence evolved into a grand Gothic castle

Wawel Hill lit up at night

complex encircled by imposing defensive fortifications and towers that was subsequently extended by King Władysław II Jagiełło (1386–1434).

Fire and reconstruction

The castle was ravaged by fire in 1499, but some of its Gothic elements, such as the Kurza Stopa (Hen's Foot Tower), survived and were later incorporated into a larger castle constructed by King Zygmunt Stary (Sigismund the Old) in 1506–35. He wanted a palatial residence and he certainly succeeded in creating one. The castle is perfectly proportioned; its beautiful three-storey, arcaded courtyard is one of Europe's finest examples of Renaissance architecture.

The designs were initiated by the esteemed Italian architect Francisco the Florentine and, in 1516, continued by another Italian architect, Bartolomeo Berrecci. The castle was finished in 1536, but a series of subsequent fires meant refurbishment was required to repair the structure; in 1595, Giovanni Trevano introduced the early Baroque elements and two additional towers.

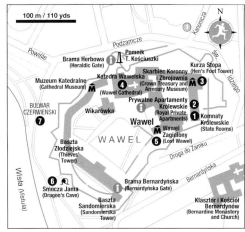

Invasion of the Swedes

Warsaw was declared the capital of Poland in 1596, and King Zygmunt III Waza (1587–1632) transferred the royal residence to Warsaw's Royal Castle in 1609. Though Wawel's importance was diminishing, it remained the site of the royal treasury and continued to hold coronations and royal funerals.

Wawel was ravaged and looted during the Swedish invasion of 1665–7, and the castle torched by Swedish soldiers in 1702. In the 1780s, King Stanisław August Poniatowski commissioned the Italian architect Dominik Merlini to oversee the refurbishments, introducing Neoclassical elements. The partitions of Poland at the end

of the eighteenth century saw the Prussians, then the Austrians, loot the royal treasury. Austria turned the castle into a military barracks.

Twentieth-century Wawel

It wasn't until 1905 that Austrian troops left the castle and renovations could begin. Work was still in progress when the Germans invaded in 1939. The main body of the castle had opened as a museum when Poland regained independence in 1918. Many of the castle's treasures were shipped to Canada during the first few days of the invasion, thus denying the Nazis some handsome booty. The castle and cathedral became a museum again in 1945.

Wawel Castle

From the main Wawel courtyard, walk past the cathedral and through the alleyway leading into a second courtyard, known as the Castle Courtyard. In the far, southeastern corner is the entrance to the **State Rooms and Royal Private Apartments** (Reprezentacyjne Komnaty i Prywatne Apartamenty Królewskie; admission to Royal Private Apartments in groups of up to ten).

State Rooms

The castle's **State Rooms** ❶ (Komnaty Królewskie), spread over the ground and second floors, may be viewed without a guide, though it is best to follow the 'suggested' route. This takes you through the former **Governor's Suite** on the ground floor, the highlight of which is the reception room, whose original sixteenth-century furniture and decor remain. The Baroque tapestries that adorn the walls are of particular note. Climbing the **Deputies' Staircase** to the second floor, you will emerge in the Tournament Hall, which has impressive Italian furniture brought from Siena.

The adjoining **Audience Hall** (Sala Poselska) is perhaps the most famous in the castle. Also known as **Hall under the Heads** (Sala Pod Głowami), it is notable for its ceiling adorned with thirty sculpted heads of kings, knights, burghers and allegorical and mythical figures; the thirty heads are all that remain of 194 originally commissioned by Zygmunt Stary.

Walk back past the staircase to the **Hall Under the Eagle** (Sala Pod Orłem), showcasing royal portraits such as Rubens's *Elizabeth of Bourbon* (1629). The **Hall Under the Birds** (Sala Pod Ptakami) is where King Zygmunt III Waza received foreign delegations – note the royal crest on a sixteenth-century wall-hanging and on the stone portal.

Next door is the castle's largest hall, the **Senators' Hall** (Sala Senatorska), which served as the

Sigismund's Chapel is crowned by a gilded dome

home of the Senate. It displays an impressive tapestry, one of a magnificent collection of wall-hangings commissioned in the mid-sixteenth century by King Zygmunt Stary (and later by his son, King Zygmunt August) and displayed throughout the castle. Of the original 360, only 142 survived the Nazis.

Royal Private Apartments

On leaving the Senators' Hall, you need to return to the ground floor to pick up the guided tour of the sumptuous **Royal Private Apartments ❷** (Prywatne Apartamenty Królewskie), which are in fact located on the first floor. The tour passes through various Renaissance and Baroque apartments, including the **King's Suite**, of which the highlight is his office, featuring rich sixteenth-century stucco decoration. Two dark, windowless rooms lead off from here, in the so-called **Hen's Foot Tower** (Kurza Stopa): their purpose is unknown, but they may well have been prisons.

The **Guest Bedroom** features the oldest tapestry in the castle, from the fifteenth century, and a late Renaissance English-style fireplace. The Italian paintings are all part of the magnificent **Lanckoroński Collection**, once held in the Lanckoroński Palace in Vienna (the Lanckorońskis were wealthy Cracovians who moved to Vienna after Poland's partition in 1795). After the fall of Communism in Poland, the Countess Karolina Lanckorońska donated the collection to Wawel's museum authorities.

Treasury and armoury

As you leave the Royal Private Apartments, the entrance to the **Crown Treasury and Armoury Museum ❸** (Skarbiec Koronny i Zbrojownia) is on your right, on the same side of the courtyard, housed in a Gothic part of the castle. The thirteenth-century *szczerbiec* ('jagged sword'), used at Polish coronations from 1320, is one of the most important exhibits of coronation regalia and medieval sacral art.

The **Museum of Oriental Art** (Sztuka Wschodu) brings together Turkish pavilions, armour, rugs and porcelain, some of which was taken as booty after the Battle of Vienna.

Wawel Cathedral

As the scene of royal coronations, weddings, funerals and state occasions, **Wawel Cathedral ❹** (Katedra Wawelska; www.katedra-wawelska.pl) is Poland's most significant church. A set of prehistoric bones by the entrance portal has hung here for centuries. Local superstition holds that the bones are those of a dragon that terrorised the city from its cave beneath the castle; only while the bones remain in place will the

Stained-glass window in the cathedral

cathedral be safe. The scientific verdict links them to prehistoric mammals.

The interior

The cathedral was built on the site of two Romanesque churches. It blends Gothic, Renaissance and Baroque, but also has some Secessionist windows by Józef Mehoffer. Entering through the main entrance, ahead of you is the Baroque main altar, which dates from the mid-seventeenth century and features an emotive painting of the Crucifixion.

Taking a clockwise route around the cathedral you will pass a total of eighteen impressive side chapels dating from the fourteenth to eighteenth centuries. The most spectacular one, **Sigismund's Chapel** (Kaplica Zygmuntowska, 1519–33), the fourth on the right, was designed by Santi Gucci, Padovano and Berreccio.

It is regarded as one of the finest examples of Renaissance sacral art in Europe. Crowned by a gilded dome, using 50kg (110lbs) of gold leaf, the chapel is the Jagiellonian dynasty's mausoleum.

Royal tombs

At the head of the church is the **Stefan Batory Chapel**, opposite which are the **royal tombs**. The earliest is the sarcophagus of King Władysław Łokietek (1333). The highly ornate tomb of St Stanisław,

Poland's patron saint, with bas-reliefs depicting his life, dates from 1671 and was sculpted in Gdańsk. The bishop was murdered in 1079 on the orders of King Bolesław the Bold, who didn't appreciate the bishop's criticisms of his immoral lifestyle.

Opposite, in a Baroque altar from 1745, is the **Cross with the Black Christ** (Czarny Krucyfiks). It was brought to Poland by Queen Jadwiga, who left her native Hungary in 1384 aged 10. She was canonised by Pope John Paul II in 1997 for her endless charitable work and for promoting Christianity in Poland.

The crypt

More royal tombs, as well as those of renowned Poles such as the poets Adam Mickiewicz and Juliusz Słowacki, Tadeusz Kościuszko (who led the 1794 uprising), and the twentieth-century statesman Marshal Józef Piłsudski, can be seen in the **crypt**, accessed via an entrance to the left of the main altar. More recently, President Lech Kaczyński was controversially interred here after the 2010 plane crash that killed many of Poland's political and military elite.

The first section, known as St Leonard's Crypt, is a prime example of Romanesque style. This is where the newly ordained Fr Karol Wojtyła (subsequently Pope John Paul II) celebrated his first Mass on 2 November 1946. As

The Envoys' Chamber, Wawel Castle

Bishop of Kraków he presided over Wawel Cathedral for ten years.

Sigismund's Bell

The largest bell in Poland, rung only on special occasions, **Sigismund's Bell** (Dzwon Zygmunta), in the cathedral's **Sigismund's Tower** (Wieża Zygmuntowska; open same times as cathedral), was cast in 1520 and weighs almost thirteen tonnes. Climbing the tower's staircase is tough going, but worth the exertion.

According to legend, touching the bell's clapper with your left hand will grant you a wish.

Cathedral Museum

Opposite the cathedral entrance is the **Cathedral Museum** (Muzeum Katedralne) established by the late John Paul II when he was Archbishop of Kraków. Here, you can see a small curated collection of twelfth- to eighteenth-century sacral art and relics.

Lost Wawel

Across the garden from the cathedral, housed within the former royal kitchens and coach house, **Lost Wawel 5** (Wawel Zaginiony) includes a display of interesting archaeological and architectural remains, such as Gothic tiles and the rotunda of the Church of the Blessed Virgin Mary, one of the earliest buildings on Wawel Hill.

Sigismund's Bell

Food and drink

1 Art Restauracja
Ul. Kanonicza 15;
www.artrestauracja.com
Set in a lovely historic house in the vicinity of Wawel Hill, this atmospheric restaurant offers a contemporary take on traditional Polish dishes. €€€

Sandomierska Tower

For a fine view to the south, climb the 137 steps of the Sandomierska Tower (Baszta Sandomierska) by Casimir IV Jagiellon.

Dragon's Cave

At the far end of the castle grounds are steps leading down to the **Dragon's Cave 6** (Smocza Jama), thought to be one of several beneath Wawel Hill and once said to be home to a fearsome dragon. At the exit, Bronisław Chromy's dragon sculpture breathes real flames at set intervals.

By the river

Between Wawel and the Wisła is a small strip of parkland known as **Bulwar Czerwieński 7**, which is popular in the summer with the locals as a place to relax in the sun or take boat trips. In the high season, boats moored by the river sell food and drink.

Locals contest a game of chess

TOUR 4
Kazimierz

Explore Kazimierz, the rapidly changing historic Jewish district of Kraków, taking in an array of synagogues, a number of Jewish museums and cultural centres, and a host of cafés and restaurants.

DISTANCE: 2km (1.25 miles)
TIME: A full day
START: Tempel Synagogue
END: New Jewish Cemetery
POINTS TO NOTE: To reach Kazimierz from Main Market Square walk along ul. Grodzka, then follow ul. Stradomska until ul. Krakowska then turn left into ul. Miodowa. Many trams serve this route: nos. 8 or 13 go to the centre.

Kazimierz was founded as a town in its own right just outside Kraków by King Kazimierz Wielki (Casimir the Great), who gave the town his own name, in 1335. Although Kazimierz is known as a centre of Jewish life, it was not totally so – the district has several historic Roman Catholic churches. Kazimierz's Jewish connections date from 1495, the time of King Jan Olbracht's expulsion of the Jews from central Kraków. Many settled in Kazimierz, where they were soon joined by other persecuted Jews from across Europe.

Flourishing community

Commerce thrived and, by the sixteenth century, the town's Jewish community was one of the most prominent in Europe. Indeed, the renowned Talmudic scholar and philosopher Rabbi Moses Isserles (known as Remuh) founded his academy here. Kazimierz became a walled town, complete with gateways, town hall and marketplace in the early seventeenth century. Only at the end of the eighteenth century, when this part of Poland was annexed by the Habsburg Empire, was Kazimierz incorporated into Kraków.

The Holocaust

When Germany invaded Poland in September 1939, about 70,000 Jews lived in Kazimierz, most of whom were soon 'resettled' in other parts of the country. In 1941 the Nazis established a Jewish ghetto in Podgórze, a separate district of Kraków, into which they herded Kazimierz's remaining 20,000 Jews. The vast majority of these were subsequently murdered in

The Star of David in the Tempel Synagogue

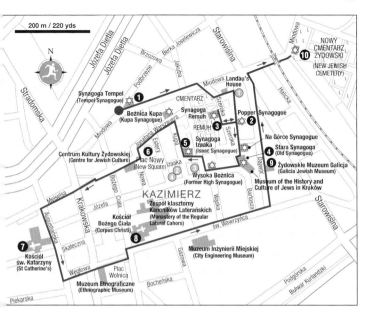

Auschwitz or other camps, and Jewish culture in Kazimierz was largely forgotten until the early 1990s.

Tempel Synagogue

At the junction of ul. Podbrzezie and ul. Miodowa you will see the Reform (rather than Orthodox) Jewish congregation's **Tempel Synagogue** ❶ (ul. Miodowa 24). Constructed in 1862, it was extended on both sides in 1924. Of the few houses of Jewish prayer in Kazimierz that survived the Nazi regime virtually intact, this was the newest.

Beautiful interior

Whereas the facade combines neo-Romanesque with Moorish influences, the interior blends ornate stucco work, red-and-gold intricately painted walls and a set of four circular stained-glass windows. Above highly gilded galleries on both sides, the beautiful ceiling is decorated with gold stars on a light-blue background. An exhibition area includes photographs and architectural drawings of all the synagogues in Kazimierz, together with historical details.

The ornate interior of Tempel Synagogue

Across the road, beyond a courtyard, you can see the rear of the seventeenth-century **Kupa Synagogue**. The front of this building is on ul. Warszauera.

Ul. Szeroka

Continue past ul. Jakuba and turn right into **ul. Szeroka** (Wide Street) and you will be in what was once the centre of Jewish life and commerce in Kazimierz. Once again a bustling neighbourhood, Szeroka was Kazimierz's most prestigious residential street inhabited by the wealthiest families. Restoration work has preserved its Jewish character.

The substantial **Landau House** at no. 2 was built as a manor house in the sixteenth century. Overlooking a small green, it now houses the Jarden bookshop, which stocks a good range of guidebooks.

Dating from the sixteenth century, the **Klezmer-Hois** (no. 6; see ❶), a café and restaurant with rooms, occupies a building that used to house the *mikveh* (ritual baths).

Approached through a courtyard at no. 16, the **Popper Synagogue** ❷ was founded in 1620 by Wolf Popper, a wealthy merchant and financier known as Bocian ('Stork'), because of his habit of standing on one leg. Originally decorated and furnished in a lavish style, it was destroyed by the Nazis. It is now used as a cultural centre.

Remuh Synagogue

Crossing to the opposite side of the wide street, you will find that the smallest synagogue in Kazimierz, **Remuh** ❸ (ul. Szeroka 40) is not merely an historic monument – it remains the centre of the neighbourhood's Jewish life and has an active, albeit small, congregation. Remuh, which dates from 1558, was the town's second synagogue, and was originally known as the 'New Synagogue'. The founder, Israel ben Joseph, was a merchant and banker to King Zygmunt II August, and the father of the renowned philosopher and rabbi Moses Isserles, known as Remuh (1525–72).

Approach the synagogue via a small, irregular courtyard and you'll see a harmonious blend of architectural genres. The current appearance dates from the major refurbishment of the 1820s and the post-war reconstruction. A rectangular, single-aisle hall is overlooked by a women's gallery. The stone collection box by the entrance to the prayer room dates from the sixteenth century, while the altar features a plaque commemorating the spot where Remuh prayed, and there are Renaissance stone portals and Secessionist doors.

Renaissance cemetery

The synagogue has its own Wailing Wall in the adjoining **cemetery**, on the ul. Szeroka side. This was built

Remuh Synagogue dates back to 1558

with fragments of Nazi-desecrated tombstones that were too small to be reconstructed. One of two Renaissance Jewish cemeteries in Europe (the other is in Prague), it was used from 1551 until the early nineteenth century. Some seven hundred gravestones, including ornate Renaissance and Baroque examples, fill 4.5 hectares (11 acres). If you're ready for a coffee or lunch break, try **Szara Kazimierz** beside the synagogue at no. 39 (see page 121) or **Ariel** restaurant at no. 18 (see page 119).

Old Synagogue

At the southern end of the street is Poland's oldest surviving synagogue, **Old Synagogue ❹** (Stara Synagoga; ul. Szeroka 24; www.muzeumkrakowa. pl), home to the **Museum of the History and Culture of Jews in Kraków**. Dating from the early fifteenth century, this building was partly modelled on synagogues in Prague, Regensburg and Worms, which explains the Gothic facade. It was extended in the sixteenth century, when the architect Matteo Gucci of Florence introduced the synagogue's Renaissance elements. In the following century, a women's prayer room and a meeting hall for the Jewish community authorities were established on the first floor. The synagogue remained the centre of Jewish worship in Kazimierz until the Nazi invasion.

Kazimierz's revival

From the end of World War II until Poland's return to democracy in 1989, Kazimierz was one of the most deprived and dangerous areas of Kraków. Since 1989, however, Polish Jews who had emigrated have been free to return to the area either to reclaim confiscated property or simply to invest, and have driven a remarkable turnaround in fortunes. Cheap property prices at the beginning of the 1990s encouraged young Polish entrepreneurs to set up shop here, as bar and restaurant owners and shopkeepers. Students – attracted by cheap rents – soon followed. Add the lively cultural scene – which grew up around the resurrected Centre for Jewish Culture – and the area was already blooming long before Steven Spielberg really put it on the map in the film *Schindler's List*. While property prices are now among the highest in Kraków, the area is still popular with students and has retained its bohemian character.

The Nazis used it as a warehouse before destroying the interiors and roof. It wasn't until several years after the war that the ruins were reconstructed. The synagogue reopened as a museum in 1959.

The Remuh's Wailing Wall

Gravestones in the synagogue's cemetery

Museum of the History and Culture of Jews in Kraków

The museum's extensive collection provides such good explanations of the Jewish faith, its history and culture that, even if you have little prior knowledge, it is easy to understand the significance of each exhibit. Many of the religious items have been collected from other synagogues. The gallery on the first floor features nineteenth- and early twentieth-century views of Kazimierz.

A monument in front of the museum marks the site where thirty Polish men and boys were executed by Nazis in 1943. A plaque also marks the spot where Polish revolutionary Tadeusz Kościuszko rallied the Jews to join his fight for Polish independence in 1794.

Two former synagogues

To the left of the Old Synagogue is the former **Na Górce Synagogue**. Though the name's literal translation is 'Synagogue on the Hill', it actually means 'Upper Synagogue', signifying that the prayer hall was on the first floor (the ground floor housed a *mikveh*). This synagogue was known for its connection with the Kabbalist rabbi Nathan Spira.

High Synagogue

Leave ul. Szeroka by the southwestern corner and head along ul. Józefa where you will find the former **High Synagogue** (Bożnica Wysoka; no. 38) on the right, dating from the mid-sixteenth century and restored after its destruction by the Nazis in 1939. The facade features a Renaissance portal and four elegant buttresses. As at Na Górce, the prayer hall was on the first floor. The building now houses a branch of the city's conservation department and a bookshop.

Lunch options

There is no shortage of restaurants in Kazimierz, so you may have already seen one you'd like to try. **Warsztat** in ul. Izaaka has many fans, see ➋; other good choices are **Bistro Zazie** round the corner at ul. Józefa 34, see ➌, or **Singer** café, see ➍.

Isaac Synagogue

Just after the High Synagogue turn right into ul. Jakuba, then left into ul. Izaaka. Ul. Izaaka was named after Isaac Jakubowicz, one of seventeenth-century Kazimierz's wealthiest merchants and moneylenders and founder of the Isaac Synagogue. Built by Giovanni Battista Trevano in 1644, the **Isaac Synagogue** ➎ (ul. Kupa 18; currently closed for restoration) is the largest in Kazimierz, and was, by contrast to the minimalist interior you see today, also the most lavishly furnished.

Ravaged by the Nazis, the building served as a sculptor's workshop after the war, and it wasn't until 1983 that

Kazimierz is peppered with outdoor cafés

renovation work began. Nevertheless, the Baroque prayer hall retains a distinctive beauty and features fragments of recently uncovered seventeenth-century wall murals together with some stucco decoration by Giovanni Falconi. On the east wall is a stone altar tabernacle; the women's gallery features an elegant arcade of Tuscan columns. In another part of the synagogue, adjoining a photographic exhibition of pre-war life entitled 'The Memory of Polish Jews', you can see films tracing the history of Jewish life in Kraków and Kazimierz.

New Square

Turn right from the synagogue, on to ul. Kupa, and walk towards the **Kupa Synagogue** (Bożnica Kupa) at the end of the street. Turn left on to ul. Warszauera and continue for 100m/yds into **Plac Nowy** ❻ (New Square). The central small, circular building, today occupied by fast-food stalls, was once a Jewish slaughterhouse. Though its bric-a-brac and fruit and vegetable stalls remain, the square has been revived by an influx of cafés and bars.

Centre for Jewish Culture

Cross over to the **Centre for Jewish Culture** (Centrum Kultury Żydowskiej; Judaica Foundation, ul. Meiselsa 17). Established in 1993 and concealed behind the 1886 period facade of a former prayer house, the centre's motto, L'dor v'dor (Hebrew for 'from generation to generation'), emphasises its commitment to Jewish culture and continuity after the Holocaust. The centre runs a full programme of cultural and international events and also incorporates a workshop, art gallery, bookshop and café.

St Catherine's Church

Continue along ul. Meiselsa, crossing ul. Krakowska, and turn right into ul. Augustiańska for a simple snack at *Kuchnia U Doroty* (see page 120), or continue left to **St Catherine's Church** ❼ (Kościół św. Katarzyny; ul. Augustiańska 7). This prime example of Gothic architecture was founded by King Kazimierz the Great in 1349. There is a legend it was a form of penance for sentencing Fr Marcin Baryczka to death by drowning in the River Vistula. This was a classic case of shooting the messenger: the priest had committed the heinous crime of conveying the bishop's disapproval of the king's dalliances with various mistresses.

The church's interiors include Baroque details, such as the impressive altar. The cloisters of the adjoining Augustinian monastery feature remarkable frescoes from the fourteenth and fifteenth centuries. An altar dedicated to Matka Boska Pocieszenia (Our Lady the Consoler) was one of the most important sites in Poland's cult of the Virgin Mary.

The Isaac Synagogue   High Synagogue wall inscription

Ethnographic Museum

Continue along ul. Augustiańska and turn left into ul. Węgłowa, where you will shortly reach **Plac Wolnica**, the former main marketplace of Kazimierz and once an important trading point on the salt route. The square is overlooked by the **Ethnographic Museum** (Muzeum Etnograficzne; Pl. Wolnica 1; www.etnomuzeum.eu; entrance to second part of museum in Dom Esterki, ul. Krakowska 46). This is housed in a splendid early fifteenth-century building that served as the town hall of Kazimierz until 1800 and which was continually extended and restyled until the mid-nineteenth century.

The museum features a collection of folk arts and crafts drawn from villages in the regions of Kraków, Podhale and Silesia. Exhibits include paintings, sculpture and costumes, as well as naive sacred art and Christian exhibits such as Easter eggs painted with rustic motifs. Recreated interiors featuring period furniture are redolent of traditional village homes. The collection extends beyond Poland, with rarities such as late nineteenth-century Siberian fur coats and folk costumes from Belarus and Ukraine.

Church of Corpus Christi

Leave the square by the northeastern corner, where you will soon see the **Church of Corpus Christi** ❽ (Kościół Bożego Ciała; ul. Bożego Ciała 26). It is another of Kraków's beautiful Gothic churches founded by Casimir the Great. The reason behind the establishment of the church at this particular location is interesting: apparently, it was here that fleeing thieves abandoned a monstrance containing the holy Eucharist which they had stolen from All Saints' Church (Kościół Wszystkich Świętych), which no longer exists.

Building began in 1340, but Corpus Christi wasn't completed until the start of the fifteenth century, when it became the parish church for Roman Catholics living in Kazimierz. King Władysław Jagiełło invited the canons of the Lateran Order to supervise the church – their residences can still be seen across the courtyard by the entrance. Among the Gothic, Renaissance and Baroque elements of this ornate but dignified church is the Renaissance tombstone of Bartolomeo Bereccio, who designed the Zygmunt Chapel and the Gothic stained-glass windows in Wawel Cathedral. The gilded main altar includes a painting of the Nativity by Tommaso Dolabella, while the ornamental pulpit takes the form of a boat.

Galicia Jewish Museum

Turn left along ul. św. Wawrzyńca, pass the City Engineering Museum (Muzeum Inżynierii Miejskiej) and turn left into ul. Dajwór, where you will find the **Galicia Jewish Museum** ❾ (Żydowskie Muzeum Galicja; www.galiciajewishmuseum.org).

Ethnographic Museum paintings

Food and drink

❶ Klezmer-Hois
Ul. Szeroka 6;
www.klezmer.pl
The hotel café has a bourgeois
air – oil paintings, roses on each table
and comfortable sofas make for a
very pleasant scene. The restaurant
manages to be more formal and more
stylishly bohemian at the same time.
Its klezmer bands ensure a lively
evening. Jewish and Polish dishes
include excellent *chłodnik* (cold
beetroot soup with sour cream and
dill) and walnut cake. €€€

❷ Warsztat
Ul. Izaaka 3;
www.restauracjawarsztat.pl
A long pizza and pasta menu and lots
of soups and salads, mean you can
lunch here inexpensively, but you can
treat yourself with a special, such as

chicken fillet with wild mushrooms
or steak in truffle sauce. €€€

❸ Bistro Zazie
Ul. Józefa 34; www.zaziebistro.pl
A cute French-flavoured bistro
serving classic lunchtime dishes
such as beef bourguignon and
onion soup alongside some more
adventurous forays into fusion, notably
the octopus in coconut or the duck
breast in teriyaki sauce. The crème
brûlée will not disappoint. €€€

❹ Singer
Ul. Estery 20/ul. Izaaka 1;
tel: 012 292 06 22
You won't be in Kazimierz long before
you realise that swathes of lace and
old sewing machines are the default
decor. As the café that started this
craze, *Singer* has a lot to answer for,
but it's still a popular place for coffee
and cake or something stronger. €€

Supported by charitable donations, this
museum was set up to present Jewish
history and culture in a different way
and performs a valuable educational
role. At its heart is a permanent
exhibition of photographs, Traces of
Memory, taken by its founder, the
late Chris Schwartz, but it also runs
a very full programme of concerts,
lectures and workshops. Its bookshop
and café are well worth a visit, too.

New Jewish Cemetery

At the end of ul. Dajwór turn right,
crossing ul. Starowiślna, into ul.
Miodowa, and walk beyond the
viaduct to reach the **New Jewish
Cemetery ❿** (Nowy Cmentarz
Żydowsk) at no. 55. The cemetery,
established at the beginning of the
nineteenth century to replace the
Remuh burial ground, contains the
graves of many renowned Jews.

Traditional moccasins

Photographs in the Galicia Jewish Museum

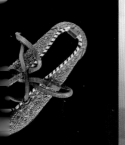

WALK 5
National Museum

This route is a visit to the National Museum, the city's largest and most comprehensive, housed in a rather stark 1930s modernist edifice, and the surrounding area west of the historic centre. For a pleasant picnic lunch, take a detour to Kraków's largest park, Jordan.

DISTANCE: 1km (0.6 mile) not including detour to Jordan Park
TIME: A half day
START: National Museum
END: Capuchin Church
POINTS TO NOTE: To reach the museum from the Old Town, take tram no. 20 three stops from Barbican (a short walk north of Main Market Square). To walk directly to the museum from Main Market Square will take around 15min.

National Museum

The **National Museum** ❶ (Muzeum Narodowe; al. 3 Maja 1) is one of the highlights of the city, housing a fabulous collection of historic works of art.

To the right as you enter the building, is the Arms and Uniforms Gallery, showcasing some 1600 military objects from the tenth to the twentieth centuries. Through a mix of video and interactive exhibits, it includes poignant memorabilia of the eighteenth- and nineteenth-century rebellions against

partition and military decorations as well as medals from World War II.

Gallery of Decorative Arts

Spanning the centuries from the early Middle Ages to twentieth-century Art Nouveau, the arts and crafts on display on the first floor detail Kraków's history as the country's centre of fine art. Here you'll find silver and gold, sacred art, clocks, furniture, fashion, glass, and a collection of ceramics that includes Polish and European decorative tiles, faience and porcelain, with examples by Meissen and Sèvres.

Twentieth-century Polish art and sculpture

Through more than four hundred works, the galleries on the second floor tell the story of the development of Polish art from the Młoda Polska (Young Poland) period. Particularly well represented is the leading talent of the epoch Stanisław Wyspiański, whose paintings combined the sensuality of Art Nouveau with the simple beauty of Polish folk art. Especially moving are

National Museum paintings

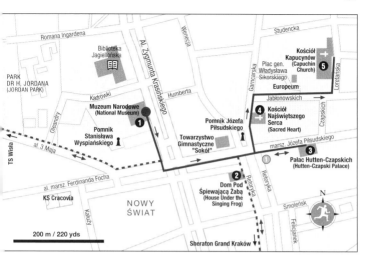

his delicate pastel portraits of wife and children. Look out for the outlandish inter-war portraits of Stanisław Ignacy Witkiewicz, popularly known as "Witkacy". Also on show are members of the avant-garde Kraków Group of the mid-twentieth century, who broke the conventions of post-war communist painting and introduced a new spirit of colour and adventure into Polish art, laying the foundations of the contemporary scene of today.

Jordan Park

A pleasant detour from the route can be made by exiting the museum through the main entrance, turning right along al. Krasińskiego, right again along al. Focha and then bearing

right along al. 3 Maja: in a couple of minutes, you arrive at the large **Jordan Park** (Park dr H. Jordana), named after a nineteenth-century Cracovian doctor, and the vast **Błonia** meadow. It's one of the few green spots in the city where picnicking is tolerated.

Ul. Marszałka Piłsudskiego

From the National Museum, take a right (passing the Wyspiański monument), then turn left at the crossroads on to **ul. Marszałka Józefa Piłsudskiego** (named after the statesman and inter-war commander). The main street of the Nowy Świat (New World) district, it is home to elegant architecture, mostly dating from the early nineteenth century.

Nothing Inside! by Jadwiga Sawicka

Morning mist in Jordan Park

Food and drink

① Pub Kuranty

Ul. Piłsudskiego 24; www.pubkuranty.pl
This renovated nineteenth-century
palace has a cellar bar-restaurant
serving a mix of Polish and Italian
dishes. The traditionally styled room
is cosy in winter, though in summer
the lack of daylight is a drawback. €€€

You'll find Towarzystwo Gimnastyczne
'Sokół' at no. 27, the gymnasium of
an organisation founded in 1867 to
promote fitness. It was a cover for the
military training of Kraków's youth
during the period of partitions.

On the corner of ul. Piłsudskiego
and ul. Retoryka is the **House
Under the Singing Frog** ② (Dom
Pod Śpiewającą Żabą). Designed by
Teodor Talowski, it is a prime example
of the neighbourhood's 'historic
revival' architecture. Next door at ul.
Piłsudskiego 30, 32, 34 and 36 are
eclectic Secessionism. Turning into ul.
Retoryka, nos. 3, 7 and 9 are Talowski
creations from 1887–91. For a break,
detour to ul. Powiśle, where the *Sheraton
Grand Kraków* is home to restaurants
and bars including **Someplace Else**
and **Anima** (see page 108).

Hutten-Czapski Palace

Further along ul. Piłsudskiego at no.
12 is the late nineteenth-century

neo-Renaissance **Hutten-Czapski
Palace** ③ (Pałac Hutten-Czapskich;
www.mnk.pl), bequeathed by
the Hutten-Czapski family to the
National Museum in 1902.

It houses the Emeryk Hutten-
Czapski Museum with a fine collection
of historic coins and notes. Taking
the form of a cube-like pavilion,
a modern annexe to the museum
contains a display devoted to the
life and work of writer, painter
and former inmate of Soviet POW
camps Józef Czapski (1893–1996).

At no. 16 is a Neoclassical
building where the novelist Henryk
Sienkiewicz, who won the Nobel
Prize for Literature in 1905, often
stayed. For a pitstop, retrace your
steps to **Pub Kuranty**, see ①.

Two churches

Head back west along ul. Piłsudskiego,
and turn right into ul. Garncarska
where the **Church of the Sacred Heart**
④ (Kościół Najświętszego Serca) at
no. 26 presents a typical combination
of a neo-Gothic facade and neo-
Renaissance and Secessionist interiors.

Turn right into ul. Jabłonowskich,
passing Plac Sikorskiego, home to
the National Museum's Europeum
permanent exhibition of European
art, and then left into ul. Loretańska.
The **Capuchin Church** ⑤ (Kościół
Kapucynów), at no. 11, was
commissioned by the Capuchin Order
late in the seventeenth century.

House Under the Singing Frog

WALK 6
Historic colleges and imposing churches

Visit some of the Jagiellonian University's historic colleges, including Collegium Maius and Collegium Nowodworskiego, and two of the city's most imposing churches, the Franciscan and the Dominican.

DISTANCE: 1km (0.6 mile)
TIME: A (long) half day
START: St Anne's Church
END: Main Market Square
POINTS TO NOTE: St Anne's Church is easy to reach from the Main Market Square: walk 250m/yds along ul. Szewska, then take a left turn through the small park.

St Anne's Church

For a flamboyant example of the Baroque style, begin at **St Anne's Church ❶** (Kościół św. Anny; ul. św. Anny 11). Modelled loosely on Rome's Church of St Andrew della Valle by Tylman of Gameren, who designed many of Poland's most beautiful Baroque structures, St Anne's was built as the university church between 1689 and 1703. The earliest reference to a church on this site dates from 1381. Its successor was a Gothic church funded by King Władysław II Jagiełło. That was in turn demolished in 1689, having become too small for the congregation.

The dome of St Anne's Church was painted by the Italians Carlo and Innocente Monti and is a rousing example of Counter-Reformation propaganda, depicting the ultimate victory of Catholicism as Christianity's one true faith. Sculptures (including one of St Anne herself) and magnificent stucco designs featuring fruit and floral motifs are the work of the Italian Baldassare Fontana.

Collegium Nowodworskiego

Across the road is **Collegium Nowodworskiego ❷** (Nowodworski College; ul. św. Anny 12), which was founded as a grammar school in 1586 by Bartłomiej Nowodworski, one of the king's private secretaries. The present building, the university's Collegium Medicum, complete with arcaded courtyard, dates from 1643 and is the oldest Polish college still in use. The actual building isn't open to the public, but there is permanent

St Anne's Church interior

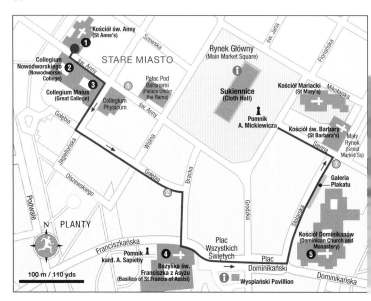

access from the street to the courtyard. For those feeling peckish the super **Chimera Salad Bar** is a 50m/yds detour from here further along ul. św. Anny at no. 3, see ①. A more substantial meal can be had at **Trattoria Soprano** (see page 118).

Collegium Maius

Pick up the walk on ul. Jagiellońska. Now a museum, **Collegium Maius** ③ (Great College; www. maius.uj.edu.pl) at no. 15 was Poland's first university college. Entrance to the courtyard is free whenever the college is open.

Collegium Maius clock

Five times a day (9am, 11am, 1pm, 3pm, 5pm), the great clock above the entrance to the museum plays the university tune *Gaudeamus Igitur* and a procession of figures from the history of Kraków appears. Though these were carved in the 1950s, the clock is ancient: a 'clock of great size' was documented as having been repaired at the university in 1465 and there are records of at least four restorations since. If you do not catch it on your walk, it is a short walk from the Main Market Square.

The college itself originated in Wawel Castle in 1364. In 1400 King

Basilica of St Francis mosaic

Władysław II Jagiełło bought a house on what is now ul. Jagiellońska from a wealthy merchant family called Pęcherz to serve as the seat of the college, then known as Academia Cracoviensis. The house was soon extended, and neighbouring houses were acquired. These buildings burnt down in the late fifteenth century, and a purpose-built college with an elegant Gothic facade took their place. Completed in 1492, when it became known as Collegium Maius, it included the arcaded cloister, from which 'professors' staircases' lead up to the professorial chambers on the first and second floors.

Professors' dining room

The professors' common room, the treasury, assembly hall and library were built in 1507–19 in Gothic style. The library features a beautifully painted skyscape on the vaulted ceiling, as well as historic portraits and various rare tomes – it became the university library in 1860. The former professors' dining room has distinctive Gdańsk cupboards and an extensive collection of gold and silver tableware.

Copernicus Room

The **Mikołaj Kopernik Room** commemorates the life of the renowned astronomer Nicholas Copernicus (1473–1543), who studied here in 1491–5, before going on to study in Bologna, Padua and Rome. His then-revolutionary theory that the sun and

Nicholas Copernicus

Polish astronomer Nicholas Copernicus (1473–1543) was the first person to formulate a scientifically based heliocentric cosmology that displaced the earth from the centre of the universe. Born in Toruń in central Poland to wealthy parents, Copernicus was by profession an economist, mathematician and diplomat. Astronomy was for him very much a hobby pursued only when time allowed, making his achievements all the more incredible. Following further study at the universities of Bologna and Padua, Copernicus did most of his astronomical observations while engaged as an administrator at the northern Polish town of Frombork. His revolutionary findings were published, in Nuremberg, just before his death.

not the earth was the centre of the universe, and that the earth and planets revolved around the sun, was set forth in *De Revolutionibus Orbium Coelestium*, which was published in 1530.

Sections of the original manuscript can be seen in the Copernicus Room, together with a collection of historic portraits, astrolabes and other early astronomical instruments. A 1510 golden globe, one of the first to show the New World, bears the inscription America, *terra noviter reperta* (America, a newly discovered land).

Collegium Maius door detail   Astrolabe in the Copernicus Room

Stanisław Wyspiański

Polymath Stanisław Wyspiański (1869–1907) was a painter, poet, dramatist, theatre reformer, stage designer and typographer. His colourful and original paintings and stained-glass window designs for the Basilica of St Francis in 1898 signalled a major breakthrough for Młoda Polska (Young Poland) – the Art Nouveau-influenced art movement that dominated Kraków in the decades before World War I. Alas, Wyspiański was as troubled as he was talented, and suffered from deep depression, often destroying recently completed work when fits would take hold. He died tragically young, of syphilis in 1907, at the age of 38. His legacy is as rich as his life was short.

Basilica of St Francis

Turn left into ul. Gołębia, where you can make for the **Gołębia 2** restaurant and wine bar for a break, see ②. Then head right into ul. Bracka, leading to the **Basilica of St Francis of Assisi** ④ (Bazylika św. Franciszka z Asyżu; entrance from ul. Franciszkańska 1, or Plac Wszystkich Świętych 5). Striking in its imposing beauty, this church was founded for the Franciscan Order, which arrived in Kraków in 1237. Designed in the form of a Greek cross, and built in Gothic style between 1252 and 1269, it was extended during the fifteenth century thanks to

King Bolesław Wstydliwy (Boleslaus the Bashful), who is buried here.

Tadeusz Popiel mosaic

The Great Fire of Kraków in 1850 destroyed some historic features and resulted in further rebuilding in a neo-Gothic style. But the church has retained historic elements, such as the Gothic galleries and fragments of wall paintings in the adjoining Franciscan monastery. By the Baroque altar, the apse features a Tadeusz Popiel mosaic depicting St Francis of Assisi. The Chapel of Our Lady the Sorrowful has a fifteenth-century painting of the Madonna, and fine polychrome.

Mehoffer and Wyspiański

The church showcases the work of two of the country's greatest artists of the Młoda Polska (Young Poland) period. The paintings representing the Stations of the Cross are by Józef Mehoffer, while the stunning polychromy on the walls and vaulted ceilings was designed by Stanisław Wyspiański. The effect of this intense combination of Gothic and floral motifs with Secessionist elements is dazzling, though it can take time to adjust your eyes to the sombre lighting. Paradoxically, the semi-darkness heightens the beauty of the stained-glass windows, also designed by Wyspiański. Stand in the main nave and look up at the window over the main entrance. Completed in 1900, it is an astonishing depiction of the Creation.

Collegium Maius assembly hall

Dominican Church

Another extraordinary ecclesiastical centre is just across the square, past the Wyspiański Pavillion (Plac Wszystkich Świętych 2), an official tourist information centre also housing stunning stained-glass panels by Wyspiański. The Basilica of the Holy Trinity, commonly known as the **Dominican Church and Monastery ❺** (Kościół Dominikanów; ul. Stolarska 12), is as austere as the Franciscan church. The church originated in 1222, when the Dominicans reached Poland. The first, Romanesque, church, destroyed by the Tartars in 1241, was greatly extended during the fifteenth century, when Renaissance elements were added. The **Chapel of St Dominic** is one of the most beautiful examples of Renaissance art in Poland, while the 1685 Rococo **Chapel of Our Lady of the Rosary** contains a painting of the Madonna copied from Our Lady of the Rosary in Rome's Basilica of Santa Maria Maggiore. You can also see the cloisters in the adjoining Dominican Monastery.

Ul. Stolarska

Ul. Stolarska, which runs up to Mały Rynek from ul. Dominikańska, was named after the carpenters who once plied their trade in workshops here. A great little café at no. 6, **Pierwszy Lokal**, see ❸, serves tea and delicious home-made cakes to tired tourists.

Food and drink

❶ Chimera Salad Bar

Ul. św. Anny 3; www.chimera.com.pl
This self-service cellar salad bar with garden is at the end of a passage off the street. Don't confuse it with the *Chimera* restaurant close by. Choose from the likes of herring salad or turkey stuffed with liver and raisins. Lovely fresh food. €€

❷ Gołębia 2

Ul. Gołębia 2; tel: 012 445 95 99
For lunching with an appetite, there are few better places than this specialist steak restaurant with meat sourced from Polish herds. It's also a great place for a relaxing glass of wine, backed by soothingly jazzy background music. €€€

❸ Pierwszy Lokal

Ul. Stolarska 6/1; tel: 012 431 24 41
Opening early for office workers who take breakfast and coffee here, this place serves as a typical Kraków café during the day before transforming into a hip and trendy bar as the sun goes down. €€

A wooden arcade on the right-hand side of the street (nos 8–10) is clustered with various specialist shops. At the end of ul. Stolarska turn left towards the Main Market Square.

The Dominican Church

The Madonna in the Chapel of Our Lady of the Rosary

WALK 7
Two historic thoroughfares

Ul. Grodzka is studded with imposing townhouses, august institutions and stunning churches; the adjoining ul. Kanonicza, one of the city's oldest and most exquisite streets, boasts several museums.

DISTANCE: 1km (0.6 mile)
TIME: A (long) half day
START: Ul. Grodzka
END: Church of the Missionary Priests
POINTS TO NOTE: Ul. Grodzka was the southern part of the Royal Route, which took kings from Florian's Gate to Wawel. Pick it up at the southeastern corner of Main Market Square. Note that this is a long route and involves walking along often very crowded, narrow streets. A good idea is to have an early lunch before heading off.

Ul. Grodzka

The long, beautiful **ul. Grodzka ❶**, leading from the Main Market Square to Wawel Castle and believed to be the site of the first Cracovian settlement outside of Wawel, is a bustling partly pedestrianised thoroughfare, with a mix of restaurants, cafés and bars, shops and galleries. Its origins pre-date Kraków's town charter: it was probably established as a main street

in the ninth century. Ul. Grodzka was traditionally known as Droga Solna (the Salt Road) because it heads off towards the Wieliczka and Bochnia salt mines. Though ul. Grodzka no longer plays host to royal processions, each year on Corpus Christi (Boże Ciało in Polish), a major parade of locals in traditional dress makes its way from Wawel to the Main Market Square.

Historic facades

Among the most attractive houses, **House Under the Lion** (Dom Pod Lwem) at no. 32 has a fourteenth-century stone lion carved above the portal. **Pod Aniołami** (*Under the Angels*) at no. 35 is a delightful, folksy Polish restaurant and café with an atmospheric vaulted cellar and a charming patio garden, see ❶.

At no. 38, **House Under the Elephants** (*Dom Pod Elefanty*) is thought to have been the residence and premises of Bonifacio Cantelli, a seventeenth-century royal apothecary. The exotic animals on the facade formed an apothecary's sign – not to be confused with the golden elephant

Elegant Grodzka Street

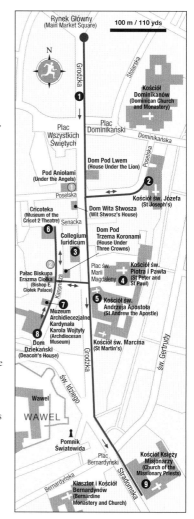

at no. 11 Plac Wszystkich Świętych. There is another excellent Polish restaurant at no. 40, **Miód Malina** (see page 116). Across the road, **Wit Stwosz's** (Veit Stoss') **House** (Dom Wita Stwosza) at nos. 39–41 was the residence of the master carver of St Mary's altar from 1478 to 1492.

Turn left into ul. Poselska and at no. 21 you'll find the Baroque **St Joseph's Church** ❷ (Kościół św. Józefa) and the adjoining Bernardine Convent.

Back on ul. Grodzka at no. 53 is the Jagiellonian University's **Collegium Iuridicum** ❸, which dates from the fourteenth century, and was restyled and extended in the sixteenth century. Originally the law school, this college now houses the university's history of art faculty. Beyond an attractive Baroque portal, you will see an arcaded courtyard.

Church of St Peter and St Paul

Opposite, at no. 54, the **Church of St Peter and St Paul** ❹ (Kościół św. Piotra i św. Pawła) is a splendid example of Baroque architecture approached through a walled courtyard set with twelve late Baroque sculptures of the Apostles. Those you see today are copies of the originals carved in the early eighteenth century. The courtyard is an aesthetic overture to a magnificent Baroque facade designed by Zygmunt III Waza's architect Giovanni Battista Trevano. Commissioned by the Jesuits, the design was modelled on

House Under the Elephants   The 12 Apostles, Church of Sts Peter and Paul

the Jesuit church of Il Gesù in Rome, following the form of a Latin cross. The impressive stucco work, at its finest in the apse, where it depicts the lives of St Peter and St Paul (1619–33), is by Giovanni Battista Falconi. This church also features a model of Foucault's pendulum, which demonstrates the rotation of the Earth.

Church of St Andrew the Apostle

Equally fine is the **Church of St Andrew the Apostle** ❺ (Kościół św. Andrzeja Apostoła), at no. 56. An early Romanesque church with a pair of elegant towers, it was founded at the end of the eleventh century and withstood the Tartar siege of 1241 thanks to its 1.5m- (5ft-) thick walls. The exquisite Baroque interior is on a far smaller scale than the facade suggests. Wall paintings by Balthazar Fontana and eighteenth-century stucco work are set between a vaulted ceiling decorated with putti and acanthus leaves, and a stunning eighteenth-century marble floor. The gilded altar is matched by a gilded limewood pulpit in the form of a fishing boat. Adjoining the church is the fourteenth-century Order of St Claire (Klasztor Klarysek), established in Poland in 1245 at the behest of Duke Leszek Biały.

Street of the Canons

Opposite the church of Sts Peter and Paul, a statue of Piotr Skarga by Czesław Dźwigaj dominates pl. św. Marii Magdaleny, which sometimes hosts art exhibitions and otherwise is a favourite with skateboarders. It leads to the tranquil **ul. Kanonicza** (Street of the Canons). This lane, lined with ornate houses and palaces, was named after the clergymen from Wawel Castle who lived here in the fifteenth and sixteenth centuries.

Buildings of note

At the northern end of the street, no. 1 has an impressive Baroque portal. The Gothic building at no. 6 once served as headquarters of Cricot 2, the experimental theatre workshop founded by ground-breaking conceptual artist and dramatist Tadeusz Kantor.

Contrast this with the Renaissance facade of the **House Under Three Crowns** (Dom Pod Trzema Koronami) at no. 7, home to *La Campana Italian* restaurant (see page 115). Look hard above the plain portal of no. 6 to see the wall painting of the Madonna of Częstochowa. At no. 18 a Renaissance doorway leads to a fourteenth-century building housing the John Paul II Institute.

At no. 17, the first of a trio of key ecclesiastical buildings, the sixteenth-century **Bishop Erazm Ciołek Palace** (Pałac Biskupa Erazma Ciołka; www.mnk.pl) has a restful courtyard, but it is worth exploring the museum here dedicated to the Art of Old Poland between the twelfth and eighteenth centuries, with some

Pope John Paul II

beautiful and simple Madonnas, while on the ground floor you will find a separate exhibition featuring many ancient icons, devoted to Orthodox Art from the eastern provinces of the Polish-Lithuanian Commonwealth.

Archdiocesan Museum

The building at no. 19 is the **Archdiocesan Museum ⑦** (Muzeum Archidiecezjalne Kardynała Karola Wojtyły). It houses a fine collection of sacred art, but many will be more interested in the replica of Pope John Paul II's study between 1952 and 1958, when he became bishop of Kraków. He then moved next door to no. 21.

This, the **Deacon's House ⑧** (Dom Dziekański) is a gem in a street rich in fine architecture. Originally late fourteenth century, it features a spectacular portal and an arcaded cloister added in the sixteenth century. The fourteenth-century house at no. 25 was once that of the medieval chronicler Jan Długosz, and later the studio of Stanisław Wyspiański's father, a sculptor.

For a well-deserved coffee break head for the fantasy-themed **Ministerstwo Tajemnic** at Kanonicxa 11, see ②.

Church of the Missionary Priests

Return to ul. Grodzka, head south in the direction of the Wawel and you'll find ul. Stradomska, a busy, gritty street with the beautiful **Church of**

the Missionary Priests ⑨ (Kościół Księży Misjonarzy) at no. 4.

The Church of the Missionary Priests was established in France by St Vincent de Paul in 1624. This particular church was built between 1719 and 1728 by Kacper Bażanka in a late Baroque style. The facade was inspired by Bernini's Sant' Andrea al Quirinale Church in Rome, while the stylised interiors were based on Borromini's work.

Ul. Kanonicza

Church of the Missionary Priests exterior

WALK 8
Matejko Square

Explore the north of the city around Matejko Square (Plac Matejki), a showpiece of late nineteenth- and early twentieth-century styles and home to some of Kraków's most notable historic buildings and ancient churches.

DISTANCE: 1km (0.6 mile)
TIME: A half day
START: Matejko Square
END: Church of the Nuns of the Visitation
POINTS TO NOTE: Leave the historic centre along ul. Floriańska, through St Florian's Gate and head past the Barbican to the square.

On the square

The central feature of **Plac Matejki** is the **Monument to the Battle of Grunwald ❶** (Pomnik Grunwaldzki). This commemorates one of the greatest battles in medieval Europe, fought in 1410 by up to 60,000 soldiers. The victory of Polish and Lithuanian armies over the Teutonic Knights effectively ended the Knights' dominance of Poland. Erected to mark the battle's 500th anniversary in 1910, the original monument was destroyed by the Nazis and reconstructed in 1976. In front of it is a memorial to the

Unknown Solider. Opposite is the Polish restaurant **Jarema**, see ❶.

Academy of Fine Arts

The square's architecture is eclectic. Its largest building is the opulent **Polish State Railways Headquarters** at no. 12 (closed to the public). Next to it at no. 13, the **Academy of Fine Arts** (Akademia Sztuk Pięknych; www.asp. krakow.pl) has a facade designed in 1879 by Maciej Moraczewski featuring a bust of Poland's great nineteenth-century painter, Jan Matejko, above the main entrance. Matejko was instrumental in establishing the academy before becoming its first rector.

St Florian's Church

In the northeastern corner of the square is **St Florian's Church ❷** (Kościół św. Floriana), traditionally the beginning of the 'Royal Way', the route by which kings of Poland entered the city to be crowned at Wawel. The church was built to house the remains of St Florian (one of Kraków's patron saints), which were brought

Monument to the Battle of Grunwald

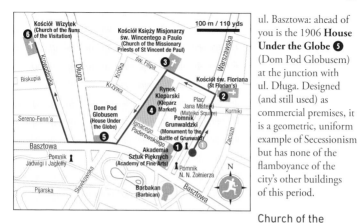

ul. Basztowa: ahead of you is the 1906 **House Under the Globe ⑤** (Dom Pod Globusem) at the junction with ul. Długa. Designed (and still used) as commercial premises, it is a geometric, uniform example of Secessionism but has none of the flamboyance of the city's other buildings of this period.

to Poland in 1184 at the instigation of King Kazimierz Sprawiedliwy (Casimir the Just). Consecrated in 1226, the Romanesque church was rebuilt several times over the centuries after Tartar sackings and fires.

Around the Square

Head west along św. Filipa. On your right at no. 19 is the **Church of the Missionary Priests of St Vincent de Paul ❸** (Kościół Księży Misjonarzy św. Wincentego a Paulo). Built in 1876–7, it was extended (in 1911–12) to include a chapel with a figure of Our Lady of Lourdes. Both this and a painting of the Crucifixion are said to have miraculous powers.

House Under the Globe

Head south past **Kleparz Market ❹** (Rynek Kleparski), and turn right into

Church of the Nuns of the Visitation

Continue along ul. Basztowa, turn right into ul. Krowoderska and you'll find the seventeenth-century Baroque **Church of the Nuns of the Visitation ❻** (Kościół Wizytek) at no. 16. The church is under the patronage of St Francis de Sales, whose mission was to provide religious education for the young.

Food and drink

❶ Jarema

Pl. Matejki 5; www.jarema.pl
Behind a charming facade, Eastern Polish cuisine dominates the menu here, including dishes from the former Grand Duchy of Lithuania (which was politically united with Poland for many centuries). €€€

House Under the Globe

Church of the Nuns detail

WALK 9
Churches of Eastern Kraków

Simply by strolling along ul. Mikołaja Kopernika (Nicholas Copernicus Street) you can see a remarkable number of beautiful and historic churches; en route you can take a break at the Botanical Gardens.

DISTANCE: 1.5km (1 mile)
TIME: A half day
START: St Nicholas' Church
END: Celestat Museum
POINTS TO NOTE: From Main Market Square walk east towards the Westerplatte to pick up ul. Mikołaja Kopernika (several trams also run along this way). Eat before setting off and bring something to drink with you, as there are no restaurants and bars en route. Don't dismiss the Botanical Gardens in the winter – the greenhouses can provide pleasant respite from the cold.

Wesoła, the name of this corner of the city, may be slowly becoming forgotten, even by locals, but the suburb is still noteworthy. Bordered by leafy trees, ul. Mikołaja Kopernika is a majestic promenade. Lined with grand houses, well-kept gardens and quiet courtyards, it was once where the city's elite lived; today it is home to some of Kraków's most revered academic institutions.

St Nicholas' Church

One of the city's oldest churches is **St Nicholas' Church ❶** (Kościół św. Mikołaja; open during services only) at no. 9. The earliest reference to this church dates from the twelfth century, before it was rebuilt in a Romanesque style in 1229. In 1456 it was taken over by the Benedictine Order. For all the Gothic restyling of the fifteenth century, and the addition of Baroque elements between 1677 and 1682, a fair number of original Romanesque sections have survived. The courtyard's medieval sculpture, known as the 'Lamp of the Dead', resembles a miniature church tower.

Society of Physicians

Opposite the church, on the left-hand side of ul. Radziwiłłowska, is Kraków's **Society of Physicians ❷** (Gmach Towarzystwa Lekarskiego; no. 14; www.tlk.cm-uj.krakow.pl). It was built in 1904 and made sublime by its interiors, many designed by Stanisław Wyspiański. Its stained-glass window featuring Apollo is one of Kraków's hidden treasures.

A superfluity of nuns near St Nicholas' Church

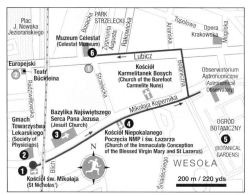

Dunikowski. Particularly dazzling are Brother Wojciech Pieczonka's series of mosaics, and the magnificent *Hołd Narodu Polskiego Sercu Bożemu* (Homage of the Polish Nation to the Sacred Heart) designed by Piotr Stachiewicz and imported from Venice.

Jesuit Church

Back on ul. Kopernika, continue under the railway bridge and look to your left. At no. 26 the **Jesuit Church ❸** (Bazylika Najświętszego Serca Pana Jezusa) is an extraordinary example of fin-de-siècle modernism, not just in terms of style, but also in scale – it's 52m (170ft) long, 19m (62ft) wide and has a 68m (223ft) high tower. First established in 1868, it evolved from a much smaller chapel. In 1893 the Jesuits decided to turn the chapel into a church that would be Poland's centre of the cult of the Sacred Heart. It was designed by the celebrated architect Franciszek Mączyński and completed in 1921.

A number of the country's finest artists and craftspeople were commissioned to work on the church. Note the entrance portal and integral sculptures by Ksawery

Bukowski murals

Vivid Secessionist murals with floral motifs by Jan Bukowski extend along a nave that's remarkable for its granite and marble pillars. The neo-Renaissance main altar, with a colonnade supporting statuary, and a mosaic extending along the apse, is highly unusual. A more recent addition is the Chapel of the Eternal Adoration of the Blessed Sacrament, completed in 1960, when the church was classified as a basilica.

Church of the Immaculate Conception

Continue along ul. Kopernika; hospital buildings line both sides of the road. On the right at no. 19, set behind a walled forecourt, is the mid-seventeenth-century Baroque **Church of the Immaculate Conception of the Blessed Virgin Mary and St Lazarus ❹** (Kościół Niepokalanego

Mosaic of Christ in the Jesuit Church

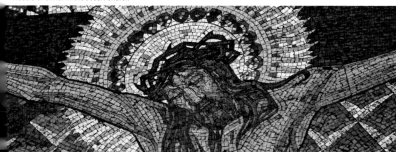

Poczęcia NMP i św. Łazarza). Since the eighteenth century, this has been the official church of the city's main hospital. Its most fascinating feature is a remarkable vaulted ceiling, painted a vivid blue. The adjacent monastery houses one of the wards of the University Hospital.

A little further along on the right at ul. Kopernika 44 is the Church of the Barefoot Carmelite Nuns (open only during services), a small convent church worth seeing for its oversized entrance, complete with Corinthian columns and elegant Baroque motifs. The convent of the Discalced Carmelite nuns connected to the church was the scene of the tragic history of the mentally unwell nun Barbara Ubryk, who was imprisoned in her cell for over twenty years, until this particular 'skeleton' was released from the convent's 'cupboard' in 1869.

Botanical Gardens

At the end of the street, on the right at no. 27, are the **Botanical Gardens ❺** (Ogród Botaniczny; www.ogrod.uj.edu.pl). Established in 1783, they were Poland's first and among the earliest in Europe. Originally comprising 2.5 hectares (6 acres), the gardens were laid out as an English-style landscaped park in 1820. Some of the trees planted then remain in the arboretum. The gardens were extended to their current size of almost ten hectares (25 acres) after World War II, and in the 1960s lots of tropical specimens and greenhouses were added.

The gardens are an adjunct of the university, which has always emphasised its educational aspect. Many botanists have learnt their craft here, and the grounds are punctuated by statues of the country's leading figures in the field. In addition to the arboretum, there are medicinal shrubs, Alpine plants (including specimens from the Carpathian Mountains, the Balkans, the Caucasus and the Alps), ponds, pools and lawns with ornamental borders. Two palm houses feature tropical and subtropical plants.

Museum

There's a small **museum** in an attractive villa, although most exhibits are labelled in Polish only. Among the exhibits are plant specimens and old prints and maps that outline the garden's origins and evolution. One of the most notable exhibits displays 260 types of wood, culled from trees native to or cultivated in Poland.

Marksmen's Fraternity

From the Botanical Gardens, head north along ul. Botaniczna and turn left into ul. Lubicz. As you do so, glance right along ul. Lubicz and you will see the contemporary

The Marksmen's mascot

Opera Krakowska building, opened in 2008. As you walk along ul. Lubicz on the left is the **Restauracja Browarna Browar Lubicz**, see ❶. If you don't have the time to stay and eat right now, it's well worth making a reservation to sample this culinary experience another time.

On the right, just across the street is the **Celestat Museum** ❻ (Muzeum Celestat; ul. Lubicz 16; www.muzeumkrakowa.pl), situated within a park. This unusual museum recounts the history of an organisation that has been integral to the city for centuries. Still extant, the Bractwo Kurkowe (literally 'Marksmen's Fraternity') was established in medieval times to teach civilians how to wield a rifle, should they need to defend the city. The museum's collection includes portraits of champion marksmen and the club's mascot, the Silver Cockerel, which is a magnificent example of Renaissance art.

The brotherhood's Corpus Christi procession, with participants dressed in historic uniforms, is an annual highlight in the Old Town. Three weeks later, in a traditional ceremony on the Main Market Square, the outgoing king of the brotherhood ceremonially presents the Silver Cockerel to the new incumbent.

A short distance from the museum the Park Strzelecki (Rifle Marksmen's Garden) features monuments to

---

Food and drink

❶ Restauracja Browarna Browar Lubicz

Ul. Lubicz 17J;
www.browar-lubicz.com.pl
Located at the renovated Lubicz Brewery complex, this restaurant serves its unique brews alongside regional cuisine prepared using locally sourced ingredients. €€€

❷ Kossakówka

Ul. Lubicz 5; tel: 012 423 25 10
A pleasant enough place to refuel after completing this route, the *Kossakówka* restaurant at the *Hotel Europejski* is in itself something of a local historical treasure. Both the wine list and the menu have been updated and now have a modern slant, though there is little for vegetarians. €€€

---

two Polish kings: Jan III Sobieski (1629–96) and Zygmunt II August (1526–72), as well as to Pope John Paul II (1920–2005).

If you are hungry, continue west along ul. Lubicz to the historic **Hotel Europejski**, home to the elegant **Kossakówka** restaurant serving good Polish food, see ❷.

Continue west on ul. Lubicz to reach the northeastern corner of the Planty.

Botanical Gardens   Portraits of former kings of the Marksmen's Fraternity

WALK 10
Museums and galleries

A look at some of Kraków's more specialised museums and galleries, including the restored homes of Jan Matejko and Józef Mehoffer, modern art centres, the Pharmacy Museum and the Szołayski House Museum.

DISTANCE: 1.5km (1 mile)
TIME: A full day
START: Jan Matejko Museum
END: Józef Mehoffer House
POINTS TO NOTE: Pick up this route halfway along ul. Floriańska, a short walk from either Main Market Square or Florian's Gate. The time it takes to complete will depend greatly on how much time is spent in each museum: to see each one properly a full day will be required, though by speed-viewing the exhibits a half day may prove sufficient. Note that most museums mentioned are closed Mondays.

By any standards, Kraków is well served by museums. These range from the vast National Museum (see page 52) to a series of fascinating mini-museums designed to document specific themes, historical eras and celebrated artists.

Jan Matejko Museum

For much of the nineteenth century, ul. Floriańska was the city's busiest street. Now closed to all but very limited traffic, it was the first street in Kraków to get a tramline (1881), which ran from the railway station to Main Market Square. You can take a coffee on this street at the historic **Jama Michalika** café at no. 45, see ➊, then make your way a couple of doors down to the **Jan Matejko Museum** ➊ (Dom Jana Matejki; www.mnk.pl). First opened to the public in 1896, this is Poland's oldest biographical museum. Popularly considered the greatest artist in the country's history, Matejko (1838–93) spent most of his life here. Illustrating the great events and personalities of Polish history, Matejko's oeuvre continues to have considerable emotional resonance. Active at a time when Poland was partitioned and thus didn't officially exist, Matejko became an important symbol of Polish identity.

Matejko's home

Though the museum preserves the atmosphere of a private home, with

Nicholas Copernicus by Jan Matejko

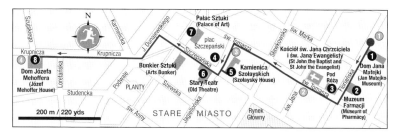

rooms furnished as they were when Matejko lived here, the restoration of the fifteenth-century building before its re-opening uncovered some previously unseen wall paintings, and multimedia installations have been added that aim to give visitors a better insight into Matejko as man and artist – particularly in his third-floor studio, where the exhibition drawn from his historical paintings underlines his influence on how Poles thought of their past and themselves.

The grand first-floor salon overlooking ul. Floriańska contains neo-Renaissance furniture commissioned by the artist in Venice in 1878. There is a cabinet displaying some of his many awards, a beautifully painted skyscape ceiling in his bedroom and several self-portraits. Matejko's designs for the wall paintings in the Mariacki church are on display, as are his collections of antique military and architectural pieces, mementoes such as his palette, spectacles, chess set and walking stick, and a wooden horse complete with a ceremonial saddle on which his subjects could pose.

Museum of Pharmacy

You will find more than a simple history of chemists' shops at the **Museum of Pharmacy** ❷ (Muzeum Farmacji), a little further on down the street near the intersection with ul. św. Tomasza. The museum occupies an elegant townhouse with a Renaissance portal, as well as Gothic and Baroque elements, and its decorative interiors and objects are worth seeing in their own right.

Cellars

In the museum's cellars you will find antique distillation equipment that might have been used by an alchemist. Indeed, legend has it that Dr Faust once studied at the Jagiellonian University, which is patron of this museum.

The wine barrels on display here recall a time when, in the belief that alcohol promoted longevity and youthfulness, Polish apothecaries

Bust of Jan Matejko on the Palace of Art

sold Italian and Hungarian wines – and, this being Poland, vodka – for supposed medicinal purposes. Red wine was thought to be particularly beneficial.

First floor

The beautiful nineteenth-century stained-glass window on the first-floor landing picturing a pestle, mortar and various herbs was taken from a chemist's shop in the city. The portrait gallery depicts various renowned apothecaries, while the reconstructed interiors include superb neo-Baroque and Biedermeier examples of nineteenth-century pharmacies.

A remarkable collection of porcelain and glass urns, used by apothecaries to store ingredients such as preserved leeches, snakes and mandrakes, as well as less stomach-turning cures and treatments, is complemented by the calm calligraphy of handwritten prescriptions.

Pod Różą

Across the road, on the corner of ul. św. Tomasza, is the **Hotel Pod Różą** ❸ (see page 106), one of the most historic in the city. Its fine guest rooms were once the stamping ground of Franz Liszt, among other notables. The **Pod Różą** restaurant, located in an attractive glass-covered courtyard, serves a menu of very good Polish-International cuisine paired with an excellent wine list.

Plac Szczepański

Walk a further 300m/yds along ul. św. Tomasza passing the Church of the Sts John (see page 37) on your right and the **Boccanera** restaurant, see ➋, on your left, and you arrive at **Plac Szczepański** ❹ (Szczepański Square), named after the Baroque Kościół św. Szczepana (Church of St Stephen). Built by the Jesuits in the thirteenth century, the church was demolished at the end of the eighteenth century.

The square has now been completely renovated and what was formerly an eyesore and a permanent car park is now traffic free. The highlight is the fountain with numerous spurting jets, providing an attractive playground for children in the summer. The square has now become a popular meeting place and somewhere to relax and observe the surrounding buildings, which include a few attractions, including the **Morskie Oko** restaurant, see ➌, unmissable due to its huge wooden doors.

Szołaysky House

On the eastern side of the square (the entrance is round the corner on ul. Szczepańska) is the seventeenth-century **Szołaysky House** ❺ (Kamienica Szołayskich; www.mnk.pl), showcasing a substantial collection of Polish design through the ages, with a fascinating array of furnishings and domestic utensils.

Hotel Pod Różą

There is also a room devoted to Feliks Manggha Jasieński (1861–1929), the art critic and collector famous for introducing Oriental art to the Kraków public – his enthusiasm had a huge influence on the Młoda Polska (Young Poland) generation. Jasieński opened his private collection of artworks to the public, laying the foundations of the National Museum's own collection. The Szołaysky House also hosts a programme of changing exhibitions.

Stary Teatr

On the corner of the square, at the junction with ul. Jagiellońska, you'll come across **Stary Teatr** ❻ (Old Theatre; ul. Jagiellońska 5; www.stary.pl), the city's – and Poland's – oldest public theatre, established in 1799 by the renowned actor Mateusz Witkowski. In its mid-nineteenth-century heyday, Helena Modrzejewska starred here before treading the boards in Warsaw and the US. In more modern times, plays here have been directed by the Oscar-winning filmmaker Andrzej Wajda – of *Katyn* (2007) and *The Promised Land* (1975) fame. The theatre was refashioned with wonderful Secessionist details in 1903 by the architects Franciszek Mączyński and Tadeusz Stryjeński, members of the Młoda Polska movement. After suffering several setbacks in the last century, it is

The Stary Teatr

beautifully restored and again a vibrant part of Kraków's cultural life.

Another example of Secessionism is the apartment at ul. Jagiellońska 2, built in 1909. A metalwork wreath crowns a stained-glass panel, with decorative balconies overlooking the square.

Palace of Art

Back on Plac Szczepański, two neighbouring buildings hold exhibitions of modern and contemporary art within very different settings. The aesthetic option is **Palace of Art** ❼ (Pałac Sztuki; pl. Szczepański 4), a Secessionist building designed by Franciszek Mączyński, with a

Plac Szczepański

Inside the J. Mehoffer House

Palace of Art

highly decorative frieze by symbolist painter Jacek Malczewski that includes busts of Matejko and Wyspiański. Apollo's huge radiant head tops the front of the building above the monumental entrance.

Arts Bunker

Built in 1968, the aptly named Arts Bunker (Bunkier Sztuki; Plac Szczepański 3a; www.bunkier.art. pl) is the only intrusion of Brutalist architecture in the city's historic centre. Designed by architect Krystyna Tołłoczko-Różyska and opened in 1965, it is nowadays considered a masterpiece of modernist functionalism, although it wasn't always so popular. Owing to its grey

concrete walls and ungainly shape the structure was soon dubbed the 'bunker'. In the mid-1990s this rather pejorative label was gleefully embraced by the exhibition hall's managers who turned their 'Bunker of the Arts – The Contemporary Art Gallery' into a stronghold of the avant-garde. It has a thriving, varied and interesting programme of contemporary art exhibitions. Every third year the gallery serves as a main exhibition venue for the International Print Triennial, one of the world's biggest festivals of print arts. The Arts Bunker has an excellent bookshop, stocking reference books on contemporary Polish art and artists, plus prints, postcards and posters.

Józef Mehoffer House

Continue west across the Planty and along ul. Krupnicza to reach the **Józef Mehoffer House ❽** (Dom Józefa Mehoffera; ul. Krupnicza 26; www.mnk.pl). One of Poland's finest painters, Mehoffer (1869–1946) was a pupil of Matejko and, together with Stanisław Wyspiański, a leading light of the Young Poland movement. In addition to landscapes, portraits and still life, he is known for his stained-glass windows.

Period interiors

The house is as notable for its stylish period interiors as for the abundance of Mehoffer's works.

Arts Bunker

Food and drink

1 Jama Michalika
Ul. Floriańska 45
Open for over a century, this café was one of the main meeting places of the Młoda Polska (Young Poland) art movement. Almost all the decor is original, from the stained-glass windows to the artworks on the walls. Even the green balloon that gave its name to the Zielony Balonik cabaret is here. €€

2 Boccanera
Ul. św Tomasza 15
The industrial decor creates a surprisingly homey atmosphere in this Italian restaurant. Delicious favourites, including antipasti, minestrone, risotto, pizza and pasta, are all available. €€€

3 Morskie Oko
Pl. Szczepański 8
This restaurant has tried to save people the trouble of going to Zakopone by bringing the mountains to the people. Expect plenty of game, mountain stews and rich broths accompanied with lashings of smoked pork fat. Hunting trophies adorn the walls amid the rustic, mountain lodge décor, and raucous live folk music adds to an enjoyable experience. €€€€

4 Dynia Resto Bar
Ul. Krupnicza 20
An Italian-themed restaurant and café offering excellent soups, imaginative pasta dishes and tempting desserts in bright, contemporary surroundings. The walled garden at the back comes into its own in summer. €€€

The artist bought the house in 1932 and most of it is furnished as it was in his day. The elegant dining room features charcoal portraits and architectural drawings of Kraków. In the library hangs a 1943 painting of the garden he created. The salon has a collection of family portraits, and there are two vast designs for stained-glass windows over the staircase. Secessionist furnishings include linen curtains embroidered with butterflies in Mehoffer's bedroom. By contrast, a Japanese room with

scarlet walls and lacquered cabinets is a treasure trove of objets d'art.

The restored garden, carefully replicating Mehoffer's original, is a delightful place to sit or stroll in summer, when the museum's *Meho Café* puts out extra tables to serve snacks and drinks. Small-scale concerts are occasionally held in the garden.

Almost next door to the Mehoffer House at Krupnicza 20, the **Dynia Resto Bar** is a handy place to wind up for food and drink, see 4.

Inside Szołaysky House

Stained glass at the J. Mehoffer House

WALK 11
Green Kraków

Escape the busy streets of the Old Town by circumnavigating Kraków's green belt. Follow the route of the old city walls, enjoy landscaped gardens and fine statuary, and duck down quirky little side streets.

DISTANCE: 5km (3 miles)
TIME: A full day
START/END: Obelisk Floriana Straszewskiego
POINTS TO NOTE: Start by the subway leading to the Planty gardens from the main railway station. This is a long walk, but there are plenty of benches along the way, if you're in need of breaks.

The **Planty** is a series of individual landscaped gardens forming a green horseshoe around the city. Short on flowers, but big on shaded avenues, lawns, water features and monuments, the gardens were created during the 1820s when the Austrian authorities demolished the medieval city walls. Foundations of the walls can still be seen on this walk, along with plaques showing where bastions once stood.

Northern Planty

On the left of the railway station subway is the **Obelisk Floriana Straszewskiego ❶**, honouring the nineteenth-century senator instrumental in planning the layout of the gardens.

Victims of Communist Provocation

From the obelisk, continue along the main footpath towards the Barbican, and you will pass a smaller monument dedicated to **Victims of Communist Provocation ❷** (Ofiarom Komunistycznej Prowokacji). Unveiled in 1936, it depicts trade union members clashing with the police. Removed by the Soviets, it was restored in 1989.

Through the trees on the left is the flamboyant late nineteenth-century **Juliusz Słowacki Theatre** (Teatr im. J. Słowackiego, see page 122), one of Kraków's leading theatres, modelled on the Paris opera house.

Barbican

Walk another 150m/yds, passing Florian's Gate (see page 35) on your left, and you will arrive at the **Barbican ❸** (Barbakan; www.muzeumkrakowa.pl). Having

Strolling in the Planty

undergone a ten-year restoration programme in the 1990s, the complex is one of Europe's biggest and best-preserved examples of medieval defensive architecture. King Jan Olbracht laid the foundation stone of this circular Gothic building that has walls up to 3.5m (11ft) wide at the base. It was surrounded by a deep moat more than 25m (82ft) wide, and linked to Florian's Gate by a bridge. You can walk around the battlements for fine views across the Planty and the interior courtyard.

Adjoining the final section of the city walls is the rear of the **City Arsenal** (Arsenał Miejski), now part of the Czartoryski Museum (see page 36).

Water features and monuments

Leaving the Barbican, you'll see one of the largest of the Planty's artificial lakes on your right, where silver birch trees, ponds and a fountain create an atmospheric setting for the 1886 statue of the poet **Bohdan Zalewski**.

Crossing ul. Sławkowska, a little further along you will see another 1886 monument marking the quincentenary of the **Union of Poland and Lithuania**. Walk another 200m/yds along the path that runs parallel to ul. Basztowa and you will see Alfred Daun's statue of his muse, **Lilla Weneda**. Daun created a series of statues for Kraków's parks in the early part of the nineteenth century; his work can also be seen in Jordan Park (see page 53).

Western Planty

Just to the southeast is the junction of ul. Pijarska and ul. św. Marka. Proceed south along ul. Pijarska and turn right into ul. Reformacka, where on the right-hand side you'll find the **Church of St Casimir** ❹ (Kościół św. Kazimierza), a seventeenth-century Baroque affair with fine Secessionist wall paintings.

Cross ul. św. Tomasza to ul. Szczepańska and the corner of Szczepański Square. On the left is the Secessionist **Palace of Art** (Pałac Sztuki; see page 73); next is the 1960s **Arts Bunker** (Bunkier Sztuki), home to outstanding exhibitions of contemporary art. On the right Wacław Szymanowski's 1901 Secessionist monument to the Kraków painter **Artur Grottger** is set in a flowerbed.

By the junction with ul. Szewska, the chic and snazzy **Zalipianki Ewa Wachowicz** café has an attractive open-air terrace with views of the Planty, see ❶.

Ul. Karmelicka and the Carmelite Church

Where the main Planty path crosses ul. Szewska, a worthwhile detour can be taken along **ul. Karmelicka**, to the right. The street once formed part of the route from Kraków to

Medieval Barbican

Florian Straszewski, the Planty's founder

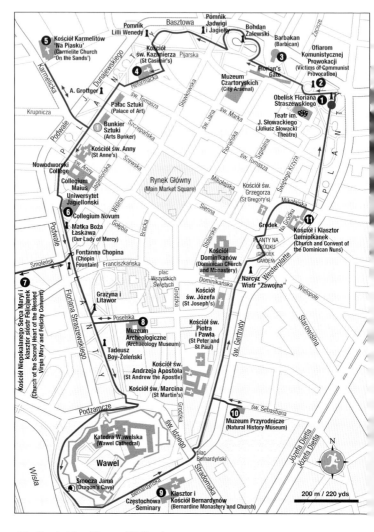

5 Kościół Karmelitów 'Na Piasku' (Carmelite Church 'On the Sands')

Pomnik Lilli Wenedy

Basztowa

Pomnik Jadwigi i Jagiełły

Bohdan Zalewski

Barbakan (Barbican)

Ofiarom Komunistycznej Prowokacji (Victims of Communist Provocation)

Kościół św. Kazimierza (St Casimir's)

Pijarska

3

Florian's Gate

2

4

A. Grottger

Muzeum Czartoryskich (City Arsenal)

Obelisk Floriana Straszewskiego

1

Krupnicza

Pałac Sztuki (Palace of Art)

Teatr im. J. Słowackiego (Juliusz Słowacki Theatre)

Bunkier Sztuki (Arts Bunker)

Kościół św. Anny (St Anne's)

Nowodworski College

Collegium Maius

Uniwersytet Jagielloński

6 Collegium Novum

Matka Boża Łaskawa (Our Lady of Mercy)

Rynek Główny (Main Market Square)

Kościół św. Grzegorza (St Gregory's)

Mikołajska

11

Grodek

Kościół i Klasztor Dominikanek (Church and Convent of the Dominican Nuns)

Fontanna Chopina (Chopin Fountain)

PLANTY NA GRÓDKU (GRÓDEK GARDEN)

7

Grażyna i Litawor

Kościół Dominikanów (Dominican Church and Monastery)

Narcyz Wiatr "Zawojna"

Kościół Niepokalanego Serca Maryi i klasztor sióstr Felicjanek (Church of the Sacred Heart of the Blessed Virgin Mary and Felicity Convent)

Kościół św. Józefa (St Joseph's)

8 Muzeum Archeologiczne (Archaeology Museum)

Tadeusz Boy-Żeleński

Kościół św. Piotra i Pawła (St Peter and St Paul)

Kościół św. Andrzeja Apostoła (St Andrew the Apostle)

Kościół św. Marcina (St Martin's)

Podzamcze

10 Muzeum Przyrodnicze (Natural History Museum)

św. Sebastiana

Katedra Wawelska (Wawel Cathedral)

Wawel

plac Bernardyński

Smocza Jama (Dragon's Cave)

9 Klasztor i Kościół Bernardynów (Bernardine Monastery and Church)

Częstochowa Seminary

200 m / 220 yds

Alfred Daun's statue of his muse, Lilla Weneda

Łobzów (today a suburb of Kraków). It was for a time one of the finest streets in the city, and though its smart nineteenth-century town houses are today a little faded (and long since divided into smaller flats), they retain a latent elegance.

The Baroque **Carmelite Church 'On the Sands'** ❺ (Kościół Karmelitów 'Na Piasku') is found at no. 19, 300m/yds along ul. Karmelicka. The church is home to the seventeenth-century painting of *Our Lady of the Sands*, hence its name. According to legend, the Virgin Mary pointed out this site to an eleventh-century Polish duke, who rubbed sand here into his body, curing his skin disease.

Collegium Novum

Picking up the main route again at ul. Szewska, pass St Anne's Church (see page 55) and Collegium Nowodworskiego (see page 55) on your left, and follow the Planty path as it darts south. In front of Collegium Maius (see page 56), by ul. Gołębia (Pigeon Street), you'll find a small wooded enclave with a statue of Copernicus dating from 1900.

Cross the square and a Matejko portrait of Copernicus (see page 70) can be seen in the assembly hall of the adjacent **Collegium Novum** ❻ (ul. Gołębia 24), like Collegium Maius part of the Jagiellonian University. This neo-

Gothic building, which was designed by Feliks Księżarski and built in 1883–7, replaced the Jerusalem College. Its facade features the university crests, and the building is now used as its main administrative centre.

In 1939 the Nazis arrested 183 academics here in a bid to destroy the city's intellectual elite: many died in Sachsenhausen concentration camp. The university counts King Jan III Sobieski and Pope John Paul II among its alumni.

Church of the Sacred Heart

Continuing in a southerly direction, you will see the joyful Baroque statue of Our Lady of Mercy (Matka Boża Łaskawa) clutching a handful of broken golden arrows. Turn right into ul. Smoleńsk, where after 100m/yds you will find the 1884 **Church of the Sacred Heart of the Blessed Virgin Mary** ❼ (Kościół Niepokalanego Serca Marii), at no. 6.

Towards Wawel

Returning to the main route, walk along the leafy Planty lane for 250m/yds, passing Maria Jarema's incongruously modern 2007 fountain memorial to Chopin, which is supposed to resemble piano hammers striking (water) strings.

Crossing ul. Franciszkańska, look out for a path leading sharply left, which leads to a small square where an 1886 **statue of Grażyna and Litawor**

The Secessionist-style Palace of Art

(two characters from 'Grażyna', regarded as one of Adam Mickiewicz's finest poems) is surrounded by trees.

Archaeology Museum

Back on Planty lane, turn left again at ul. Poselska, and head towards the **Archaeology Museum**  (Muzeum Archeologiczne; w Krakowie, ul. Senacka 3; www.ma.krakow. pl), housed in a former friary of a Carmelite Order. Founded in 1606, this is the oldest Archaeology Museum in Poland, and contains fine exhibits, including Egyptian mummies, clothing from 70,000BC to the fourteenth century, and a rare relic of pre-Christian Slavonic culture: the tenth-century stone column of Światowid. It also has a pleasant walled garden.

Turn left from the museum and head back towards Planty, with Wawel directly ahead. You will you reach a small square containing a monument to the physician, translator and arts critic **Tadeusz Boy-Żeleński** (1874–1941).

Wawel's walls

On reaching ul. Podzamcze, turn right and trace the walls of Wawel Royal Castle all the way round, the tower of Wawel Cathedral (see page 41) visible on your left. You will pass Dragon's Cave (Smocza Jama, see page 43), after which the path forks. To follow Planty around

take the left fork. At the next fork continue straight (rather than turning left) to arrive on ul. Bernardyńska.

Bernardine Monastery

Now walk some 300m/yds along ul. Bernardyńska, passing the **Częstochowa Seminary**, built in 1928, and head for the **Bernardine Monastery and Church** (Klasztor i Kościół Bernardynów; also known as the Reformed Franciscan Church; open only for Mass), next to the seminary at no. 2. The Bernardine Order was established here in the fifteenth century by the anti-Semitic Giovanni da Capistrano. A wooden church originally stood on the site; the present, Baroque church dates from the seventeenth century. The church's *Madonna and Child with St Anne* is the only part of the wooden church that has survived. Later details include Mehoffer's stained-glass windows depicting the life of St Simon, a fifteenth-century Bernardine monk.

Eastern Planty

Leave the church, turn right and, after crossing busy ul. Stradomska, take a left before darting right at the first opportunity into the eastern stretch of the Planty.

Natural History Museum

After 150m/yds, past the *Royal Hotel*, turn right into ul. św. Sebastiana for a short detour to **Natural History**

Collegium Novum

Museum **⑩** (Muzeum Przyrodnicze) at no. 9. Established in a Secessionist former public bathhouse in 1865, the museum was recently given a makeover. Top billing still goes to the world's only stuffed prehistoric woolly rhinoceros. Other exhibits include exotic animals, the evolution of crabs, the rainforest and many activities to engage children.

Returning to the Planty path you can see that the churches of St Andrew the Apostle (see page 62) and Sts Peter and Paul (see page 61) are almost as impressive from the rear as from the front, as you walk north along the tree-lined lanes towards St Joseph's. Crossing ul. Dominikańska, with the Dominican Church (see page 59) on your left, you will soon pass a statue of **Narcyz Wiatr Zawojna**, a Polish colonel shot by the Soviets in 1945.

Church of the Dominican Nuns

Crossing ul. Sienna and entering the **Gródek Garden** (Planty Na Gródku), turn left and follow the curve of ul. św. Krzyża. As ul. św. Krzyża crosses ul. Mikołajska, you will see the entrance of the **Church and Convent of the Dominican Nuns ⑪** (Kościół Matki Boskiej Śnieżnej i Klasztor Dominikanek; open only for Mass) at no. 21.

Founded by Duchess Anna Lubomirska in the 1630s, it possesses elegant Baroque interiors, with an

Food and drink

① **Zalipianki Ewa Wachowicz**
Ul. Szewska 24; www.zalipianki.pl
This design-conscious café serves a fine selection of snacks, cakes, bite-sized sandwiches and teas as well as some very strong coffee. Perfect for a break while exploring Planty Gardens. €€

ornamental vaulted ceiling, a neo-Baroque main altar and a celebrated seventeenth-century painting, *Matka Boska Śnieżna* (*Our Lady of the Snow*), a gift from Pope Urban VIII, said to have miraculous powers of healing.

Just east across ul. Na Gródku is the *Gródek Hotel*, whose restaurant **Restauracja Gródek** (see page 105), is a good choice for dinner.

From the convent, return to ul. Mikołajska and head north along the Planty path to reach the Florian Straszewski Obelisk. Shoppers might want to end the walk with a trip to the Galeria Krakowska (ul. Pawia 5; www.galeriakrakowska. pl), the city's largest shopping mall, which is full of international brands and can be reached via the subway leading to the railway station (between the station and the main post office). The shopping mall is well equipped with plenty of fast-food outlets, bakeries and cafés.

Wawel Cathedral and Castle

Bas-relief of the Częstochowa Seminary

WALK 12
Podgórze: the Jewish Ghetto

Visit the site of Kraków's former Jewish ghetto, which for two years during World War II was a place of horrific suffering and brutality. Overlooked for decades, its historical importance is only now being fully recognised.

DISTANCE: 3.5km (2.25 miles)
TIME: A half day
START: Plac Bohaterów Getta
END: Schindler's Factory
POINTS TO NOTE: Tram 13 runs from Poczta Główna on the edge of the Old Town through Kazimierz and over the Wisła (Vistula) River into Podgórze. To follow the route taken by the Jews when the Nazis created the ghetto in 1941, walk over the Most Powstańców Śląskich.

On 3 March 1941 the Nazis set up a Jewish ghetto in Kraków's Podgórze district and herded into it the 20,000 Jews from Kazimierz who had not already been sent to concentration camps. Forced to leave at less than a day's notice, they were allowed one cartload of possessions per family, and were crowded into 320 buildings between Plac Bohaterów Getta and Rynek Podgórski. From here, they were sent to Auschwitz or Płaszów. Of the almost 70,000 pre-war Jewish population of Kraków, only around two thousand survived.

Heroes of the Ghetto Square

If you cross Powstańców Śląskich Bridge on foot you will arrive at **Plac Bohaterów Getta ❶** (Heroes of the Ghetto Square). Once the centre of the ghetto, it features a poignant memorial to those murdered by the Nazis, in the form of seventy randomly scattered chairs in bronze. The memorial, designed by Piotr Lewicki and Kazimierz Łatak, refers to the scene after the ghetto's liquidation in 1943, when all that remained was furniture.

Museum of National Remembrance

Ahead in the far southwest corner of the square, is Tadeusz Pankiewicz's **Eagle Pharmacy ❷**, now a museum (Apteka Pod Orłem; Plac Bohaterów Getta 18; www.muzeumkrakowa. pl). Pankiewicz was the only gentile resident of the ghetto. He operated his pharmacy throughout World War II, helping the Jews any way he could.

Chairs memorial, pl. Bohaterów Getta

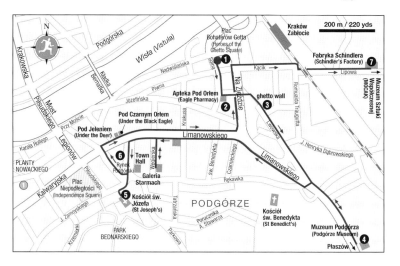

He gave sedatives to Jewish children to keep them quiet during Gestapo raids, and let the ghetto's underground movement use the pharmacy as a meeting and hiding place.

Ghetto wall

Turn right as you exit, cross ul. Na Zjeździe and head through the park to ul. Lwowska 25, where on the left is one of just two remaining sections of the **ghetto wall ❸**, which once enclosed the entire area. The small plaque reads: '*Here they lived, suffered and perished at the hands of Hitler's executioners. From here they began their final journey to the death camps.*'

One survivor of the ghetto was film director Roman Polański, who, as an 11-year old boy, escaped through a hole in the ghetto wall during its liquidation. He survived the rest of the war by hiding in the forests that surround Kraków, with the help of Polish families. In 2002 he won an Oscar for Best Director for *The Pianist*, set in the Warsaw ghetto.

Ul. Limanowskiego

Head south along ul. Lwowska until you reach ul. Limanowskiego, Podgórze's main street. Just south of here, at the top of a hill, is the eleventh-century **St Benedict's Church** (Kościół św. Benedykta).

Continue along ul. Limanowskiego for about 400m/yds until you reach the corner of ul. Powstańców

The Eagle Pharmacy   A reminder of Podgórze's history

Concentration camp

Set up in 1942 as a slave labour camp, Płaszów concentration camp was the fiefdom of Amon Göth, the brutal camp commandant portrayed by Ralph Fiennes in *Schindler's List*. Though it was not an extermination camp as such, death from disease and execution were daily occurrences, and more than 10,000 people are thought to have died here.

You can wander around the few overgrown remains of Płaszów by taking tram 13 three stops south from Plac Bohaterów Getta. Climb up the hill on foot and take a right into ul. Jerozolimska. There is a large memorial to the dead in a clearing, while Göth's crumbling former home can be seen further on at ul. Heltmana 22.

Wielkopolskich and the **Podgórze Museum** ❹ (Muzeum Podgórza; www.muzeumkrakowa.pl) which opened in the building of St Benedict's Inn in 2018. This informative museum tells the history of Podgórze and its inhabitants from the eighteenth century to the present day.

Walk back along ul. Limanowskiego until you reach ul. Węgierska on the left, where at no. 5, inside a former synagogue, is one of Poland's leading contemporary art galleries, the **Galeria Starmach** (www.starmach.com.pl).

Płaszów camp memorial

Continue along ul. Limanowskiego. You will see the monumental neo-Gothic **St Joseph's Church** ❺ (Kościół św. Józefa) to the left, at the far end of **Rynek Podgórski** ❻, Podgórze's former market square. On the eastern side of the square is the nineteenth-century former Podgórze **town hall**, next to which once stood another factory, which used Jewish slave labour.

On the square's northern side are two former inns, built in the mid-eighteenth century: **Under the Deer** (Pod Jeleniem) is at no. 12, **Under the Black Eagle** (Pod Czarnym Orłem) is at no. 13.

For a coffee break, stick on Rynek Podgórski and dive into **De Revolutionibus** at no. 8, a bookshop that also serves a mean cappuccino. For good food, however, walk a little further west, along ul. Kalwaryjska, past **Plac Niepodległości** (Independence Square) to **Ogniem i Mieczem** on Planty Nowackiego, see ❶.

Schindler's Factory

Retrace your steps to Plac Bohaterów Getta, cross the square and head east on ul. Kącik. Continue under the railway bridge along ul. Lipowa, to no. 4, **Schindler's Factory** ❼ (Fabryka Schindlera; www.muzeumkrakowa. pl; under-14s must be accompanied by an adult). This is where Oskar Schindler first exploited and then protected and rescued more than one thousand Jews of the Podgórze ghetto.

The former administrative block is now a branch of the Historical Museum of the City of Kraków, with an exhibition of Kraków under Nazi Occupation 1939–1945. Schindler's actual office forms part of this 'Factory of Memory', which makes imaginative use of eyewitness accounts, documentary film and photographs, multimedia presentations and a Survivors' Ark, created from thousands of enamel pots. The 1993 film *Schindler's List*, directed by Steven Spielberg, is a largely faithful account of life in and around the Podgórze ghetto in 1942–3.

Next door, the former factory was transformed in 2011 into the Museum of Contemporary Art in Kraków (MOCAK, Muzeum Sztuki Współczesnej w Krakowie; www.mocak.pl), one of Poland's best contemporary art collections which also hosts international travelling exhibitions.

The smart and stylish *MOCAK Café* is the perfect place to unwind.

Food and drink

🟡 Ogniem i Mieczem

Pl. Emila Serkowskiego 7;
www.ogniemimieczem.pl
Boar and duck top the bill at this seventeenth-century huntsman's paradise decked out with trophies and animal skins. €€€

Oskar Schindler

Schindler (1908–74) was born to a wealthy family in the Sudetenland (present-day Czech Republic). He moved to Kraków at the outbreak of the war (allegedly to avoid conscription), and bought a factory, which he staffed with cheap Jewish labour. Producing bomb casings for the Nazis, he grew rich, yet he frittered away much of his money on women and black-market goods, which he used to buy the local SS officers' loyalty.

After witnessing the liquidation of the Podgórze ghetto in 1943, Schindler vowed to help 'his' Jews, and managed to declare his factory a sub-camp of Płaszów concentration camp. As the Red Army closed in on Kraków, however, his factory was forced to close, and his Jews were slated for deportation to an extermination camp. Schindler persuaded the authorities to let him take 1200 workers to a new factory at Brunnlitz, close to his hometown.

Brunnlitz was freed by the Red Army in May 1945, though Schindler had fled the night before – a Nazi party member since 1939, he would likely have been shot. He lived in Argentina until 1958, when he returned to Germany. When he died in 1974, he was bankrupt, living off the charity of those he had saved.

WALK 12 SCHINDLER'S FACTORY

Schindler's Factory exhibit

One of the few remaining sections of the ghetto wall

WALK 13
Nowa Huta

Take a tram to Nowa Huta, a 1950s' experiment in social engineering. This town and steelworks built to an entirely Socialist Realist concept 10km (6 miles) east of the city centre was devised to redress what Poland's Communist leaders saw as Kraków's 'class imbalance'.

DISTANCE: 3km (2 miles)
TIME: A half day
START: Plac Centralny
END: Arka Pana Church
POINTS TO NOTE: To get to Nowa Huta you should take tram no. 4 from Kraków's main railway station. The journey takes no more than 35min. A taxi takes considerably less and costs around 50zł each way.

Conceived by Poland's Communist authorities in collusion with the Soviet Union at the end of the 1940s, Nowa Huta (New Steelworks) was constructed to create both a modern steelworks to support the industrialisation of southern Poland, and a proletarian base in Kraków: until then, Kraków was seen (somewhat mistakenly) as a city without a working class.

Built mainly from 1949 to 1956, the architecture of Nowa Huta is a mix of neo-Renaissance, Neoclassical and Utilitarian. Ignored by visitors for years, the town has attracted something of a cult following recently both for those interested in Communist-era history and for students of town planning. For the casual visitor it provides a telling insight into how the 'utopia' many Communists aspired to create might have looked.

Central square

If coming from Kraków by tram, get off at **Plac Centralny ❶**, the centre of Nowa Huta. All streets fan out from here, and the scene – of five almost identical, wide, tree-lined avenues and smart blocks – is immediately impressive.

Designed by a collective of Polish architects, the square was the first part of Nowa Huta to be completed, in 1956. Looking around, you will note that the southern side of the square lacks any buildings: a giant cultural centre was planned for the site but never built.

Before heading further into Nowa Huta, cross over to the southern side of the square and take a quick

Concrete colonnade on Plac Centralny

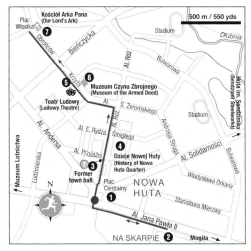

Nowa Huta's **former town hall ③**. The grand town hall designed for this square was never built and the statue of Lenin that stood here was finally removed in 1989, having survived the residents' spirited attempt to blow it up in 1979.

This is also the location of **Stylowa**, the oldest restaurant and one of the very few places in Nowa Huta to eat that isn't a milk bar, see ①.

detour east for 100m/yds along al. Jana Pawła II for a glimpse at the blocks of the **Na Skarpie ②** district. Built in the 1970s, they are considered by most to be an eyesore.

Main street

Walking back to Plac Centralny, head directly north along **al. Róż**, Nowa Huta's main thoroughfare. After 50m/ yds it widens to form a large square, often used today for concerts. The Neoclassical apartment blocks that line the square are the finest in the town and were reserved for the highest echelons of steelwork management.

The taller building on your left, on the corner of al. Przyjaźni, and sporting a rather sublime loggia, is

Cross al. Przyjaźni and detour right into one of the many little **parks** that dot the town.

Nowa Huta was designed so that a third of its area would be green space. Stroll through to the other side of the park (there are benches if you need a rest) and across to the **History of Nowa Huta Quarter ④** (Dzieje Nowej Huty; os. Słoneczne 16; www.muzeumkrakowa.pl), a small museum staging exhibitions on the town's history and culture.

Ludowy Theatre

Head north a further 100m/yds along al. Róż to the junction with al. Żeromskiego. Turn left and walk northwest, taking the right-hand fork

Our Lord's Ark Church bells

A street named after Pope John Paul II

City of rebels

Nowa Huta was designed to be a city of 100,000 of the proletariat (today's population is approximately 65,500), with its inhabitants all loyal supporters of the Communist party. Like much about Nowa Huta, however, not everything went according to plan. The workers of the steel plant have often been a major thorn in the side of Poland's authorities, both before and after the fall of Communism, most notably during Martial Law in 1981.

As Nowa Huta expanded in the 1970s, and huge tobacco and cement factories also opened nearby, new housing had to be built quickly. As a result, building standards dropped, and the size of apartments shrank. With the general drop in living standards throughout Poland in the late 1970s, Nowa Huta's workers came out on strike in support of the Solidarity movement in 1981. The authorities had to use force to quell the riots – killing a steelworks apprentice during a demonstration in 1983.

Ironically, the fall of Communism and the onset of capitalism may see the death of Nowa Huta. The steelworks face a precarious future.

after 50m/yds. On your left, set back from the street, is the **Ludowy Theatre** ❺ (Teatr Ludowy; os. Teatralne 34), a low-rise building that is one of many in Nowa Huta sadly showing signs of neglect. Completed in 1955, the theatre has long been associated with avant-garde productions.

Museum of the Armed Deed

Cross the street and the tank that faces you marks the entrance to the **Museum of the Armed Deed** ❻ (Muzeum Czynu Zbrojnego; os. Górali 23), a rather touching exhibition devoted to those from the Nowa Huta area who have fought and died for Poland.

Arka Pana

Exit the museum and turn right, walking a further 300m/yds to Plac Włosika, where you will find the startling **Arka Pana** or **Our Lord's Ark** ❼ (Kościół Arka Pana; ul. Obrońców Krzyża 1; www.arkapana. pl; closed to sightseers during Mass), the first church to be built in Nowa Huta, between 1967 and 1977.

Designing a socialist utopia meant no room for churches, and for decades the authorities refused repeated calls from locals to build one. Finally, Nowa Huta's faithful took things into their own hands and began construction of the church.

Designed by Cracovian Wojciech Pietrzyk to resemble Noah's Ark resting on Mount Ararat, Arka Pana was built brick by brick, work often stopping for months due to a lack of materials. It was consecrated in 1977 by the then Cardinal Wojtyła, soon to become Pope

Inside Our Lord's Ark church

John Paul II, who had dug the first foundations as Archbishop of Kraków ten years earlier, and helped prevent its demolition by hostile authorities.

Among the highlights inside are a huge figure of Christ flying up to Heaven by Bronisław Chromy, the tabernacle containing a fragment of rutile crystal brought back from the moon by the crew of Apollo 11 and a statue of Mary made from 10kg (22lbs) of shrapnel removed from Polish soldiers wounded at Monte Cassino.

The Steelworks

To return to Kraków's Old Town, turn left from the church, then right onto ul. Bieńczycka and up to its junction with Al. Andersa, where you can take bus 502 or tram no. 1 at the roundabout. However, for many people a visit to Nowa Huta is not complete without a trip to the town's raison d'être, the steelworks, although note that they are off limits to the public.

To get there, head back to Plac Centralny, and take tram no. 4 to the Kombinat stop, directly in front of the steelworks' entrance. You can't miss it: enormous letters framed by monumental twin buildings (the administration centre) tell you that this is **Huta im. T. Sendzimira** (Sendzimir Steelworks).

Nowadays owned by the Arcelor-Mittal group, during Communism the steelworks carried the name of Lenin, and its workers were famously

militant. At its peak in the 1970s the Nowa Huta steelworks were producing 6.5 million tonnes of steel annually. Today, output is much reduced, and it employs a little more than ten percent of the staff it once did.

Just west of Nowa Huta is the Polish Aviation Museum (Muzeum Lotnictwa Polskiego; al. Jana Pawła II 39; www.muzeumlotnictwa.pl). Highlights include the fighter aircraft designed for Poland's inter-war Airforce by Warsaw's PZL factory, a Sopwith Camel and one of the world's few remaining Spitfires in perfect condition. Lined up outside are Soviet-made MIG jetfighters, Ilyushin bombers and other example of Cold-War aerial power.

To get there take tram no. 10 to the AWF stop. If you're coming from the city centre then walk back the way you came a short distance – the museum is set back from the road through a small wooded park. If in doubt, ask a local to point the way.

Aviation Museum plane

Nowa Huta is named after the steelworks

TOUR 14
Zakopane

This is a pretty holiday resort in the Carpathian Mountains; its 27,000 inhabitants are Górale, or highlanders, and for more than a century this has been a traditional retreat for intellectuals as well as Poland's winter sports capital.

DISTANCE: 100km (62 miles) one way from Kraków; town centre tour: 3.5km (2 miles)

TIME: A full day

START: *Grand Hotel Stamary*

END: *Gubałówka*

POINTS TO NOTE: Most of Zakopane's sights can just about be visited on a day-trip from Kraków, although if you want to hike or ski then you should stay at least one night. Zakopane can be reached from Kraków by train or bus. The train ride is leisurely and highly scenic: the bus is usually quicker but can get held up by traffic during busy holiday periods. There are a number of private bus companies of varying comfort operating the route; they depart from Kraków's main bus station and deposit passengers at the *Grand Hotel Stamary*. The journey by bus takes just over two hours in good weather.

The sprawling town of **Zakopane** is known for its beautiful mountain scenery in summer and prime skiing in winter. Set at the foot of the Tatra Mountains, Zakopane was, from the sixteenth century, a village of sheep farmers. The Górale people who live here speak their own dialect and maintain traditional customs, including folk music and dancing. The local architecture is characterised by wooden buildings adorned with carvings and painted rustic motifs.

Healthy air and highland culture

Poland 'discovered' Zakopane in the 1870s, when a Warsaw doctor, Tytus Chałubiński, visited what was then a village. The first hotel was built in 1885 to accommodate artists and intellectuals attracted by the healthy mountain air and a rich folk culture that preserved many Polish traditions that the lowland cities had lost. Zakopane became a bohemian centre at the start of the twentieth century, with a guest list starring, among others, the Nobel Prize-winning novelist Henryk Sienkiewicz and the concert pianist Ignacy Paderewski. Some of

Zakopane, a quaint alpine retreat

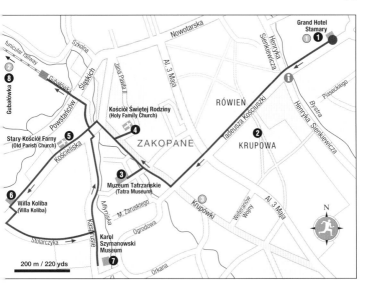

Poland's leading artists established permanent homes here, and elements of highland culture began to appear in the work of composers such as Karol Szymanowski and writers including Jan Kasprowicz. The painter, architect and critic Stanisław Witkiewicz was a key figure in propagating the 'Zakopane style' of wooden buildings; his son Witkacy had a famous portrait-painting studio here.

Town centre

Having arrived at the bus station in front of the **Grand Hotel Stamary ❶**, you might want to relax for a while in the hotel's **Café Stamary**,

see ❶. From here, turn right and head along ul. Kościuszki as it passes through the town centre's largest park, the **Rówień Krupowa ❷**.

Tatra Museum

Cross al. 3 Maja and continue to ul. Krupówki, the town's busy main thoroughfare. Turn right and walk along to the **Tatra Museum ❸** (Muzeum Tatrzańskie; ul. Krupówki 10; www.muzeumtatrzanskie. pl). Itself an example of an early Zakopane-style building, it has fine collections of folk art and natural history, and more besides: two reconstructions of

Enjoying a drink and a mountain view

Hiking and skiing

This region is popular with hikers – numerous trails lead to the gorgeous Alpine scenery of the Tatra Mountains. All routes are well marked, but you should not set off without a decent map, available at tourist information centres and good Kraków bookshops. Most of Zakopane's 3.5 million annual visitors, however, come to ski, with reliable snow conditions from December to mid-April. Note that the ski runs are split into four separate areas, none of which interlinks. When the snow is deep (more than 6m/18ft) the best skiing is on Kasprowy Wierch to the south of the resort, accessed by Poland's first cable car, installed in 1936 but now replaced with an up-to-date, high-tech version (www.pkl.pl).

ancient mountaintop dwellings delight kids of all ages.

Two parish churches

Opposite is the 1877–96 neo-Romanesque **Holy Family Church** ❹ (Kościół Świętej Rodziny). Witkiewicz designed its **Chapels of John the Baptist and Our Lady Mary of the Rosary** (Kaplica Jana Chrzciciela i Matki Bożej Różańcowej), as well as the stained-glass windows and polychromy, in the Zakopane style.

Turn right into ul. Krupówki and then left into ul. Kościeliska. On your right is the town's oldest church, the mid-nineteenth-century **Old Parish Church** ❺ (Stary Kościół Farny, also known as Kościół na Pęksowym Brzyzku). In the cemetery here you'll find the tombstones of famous figures, including Witkiewicz and Chałubiński, as well as that of Helena Marusarzówna, a Polish ski champion shot by the Nazis in 1941 for being a member of the Polish resistance.

Villa Koliba

About 100m/yds further along is the **Villa Koliba** ❻ (Willa Koliba; ul. Kościeliska 18; www.muzeum tatrzanskie.pl), built in 1893 by Witkiewicz in a design inspired by a highlander's cottage. Inside is a display devoted to the so-called Zakopane Style, the folk-influenced architecture and interior-design trend influenced by Witkiewicz's work.

Karol Szymanowski Museum

From here, cross the road and walk along ul. Stolarczyka to ul. Kasprusie. To your right, on the other side of the street, is the Villa Atma's **Karol Szymanowski Museum** ❼ (ul. Kasprusie 19; www.mnk.pl). The villa was home in the 1930s to the composer Szymanowski (1882–1937) and contains some wonderfully evocative interiors.

Tatra sheepdog

Food and drink

1 **Café Stamary**
Ul. Kościuszki 19; www.stamary.pl
After a journey from Kraków, you
may wish to refuel with coffee
and cake in this café, conveniently
located in the imposing *Grand Hotel
Stamary* beside the bus station. €€€

2 **Tarasy Gubałówka**
Ul. Droga Stanisława Zubka 6;
tel. 018 531 49 19
At the top of the Gubałówka, this
mountain retreat offers cheap
and cheerful Polish dishes and
pizza in a wood and glass building.

The views over the mountains
are terrific. On the downside, you
have to pay for the toilets. €€

3 **Karczma Sabała**
Ul. Krupówki 11;
www.sabala.zakopane.pl
Places like this are what Poland's
mountains are all about. A super
wooden villa (with hotel rooms on
the upper floors), good food, a great
atmosphere and decent prices. The
food is local: Górale specialities
such as *patelnia bacowska*, a rich
lamb stew, are a feature. The staff
are friendly and speak English. €€

Up to Gubałówka

Walking back to the town centre
along ul. Kasprusie, cross the small
park, then pass through the town's
large **market** and head up on to Na
Gubałówkę. At no. 2 is a wonderful
shop and **gallery** selling paintings
of Zakopane and its mountains
(do not expect bargains) as well
as local painted glass (the town
has a history of glass-painting).

Funicular and food

A short distance up the hill is a
funicular (www.pkl.pl), which whisks
skiers, bobsledders and hikers up to
Gubałówka 8, once a tiny mountain
village, now a mini resort-within-a-
resort. In winter there are some short
and easy ski runs from here, while in
summer there is a 750m/yd -long dry
bobsleigh run, an adventure rope park
and long hikes across the Tatras.

The **Tarasy Gubałówka Restaurant**
at the top of the funicular is a scenic
spot to eat, see **2**, or a place to rest
tired legs if you have walked up the
mountain. The route is steep – it can
be done by the very fit in around an
hour, weather-permitting, but is not
recommended for young children or the
elderly, or for anyone in bad weather.

Alternatively, head back into town
to ul. Krupówki for hearty Górale
cooking served on the first-floor, open-
air terrace at **Karczma Sabała**, see **3**.

Tatra Museum   The Old Parish Church

TOUR 15
Auschwitz

The infamous Nazi concentration and extermination camp of Auschwitz-Birkenau was the largest such complex in Nazi-occupied Europe; and also the location where the largest number of Jews were murdered during the so-called Final Solution. Now a UNESCO World Heritage Site, it is a unique, haunting and profoundly moving place, essential to our understanding of the Nazi regime's crimes.

DISTANCE: 60km (37 miles) west of Kraków
TIME: A full day
POINTS TO NOTE: Oświęcim is served by regular buses from Kraków's bus station (see www.auschwitz.org for timetables). The journey takes about 1hr 30min. Buses to Kraków depart opposite the memorial reception area. Less frequent trains from Kraków Dworzec Główny stop at Oświęcim but the station is about a 25min walk from the camp. There is a canteen at the site entrance serving drinks, snacks and some hot meals. Bring water in summer.

The town of **Oświęcim** (Auschwitz in German) will always be synonymous with the Holocaust. It is now an industrial centre south of Katowice, Poland's key industrial conurbation. The site of a castle in the twelfth century, it became the capital of an independent dukedom in 1317 and part of Poland in 1457. In the years of Poland's partition (1772–1918) the town was part of the Habsburg Empire.

Creation of Auschwitz-Birkenau
Shortly after invading Poland in 1939, the Nazis took over a barrack complex outside Oświęcim/Auschwitz and turned it into a concentration camp for (mainly Polish) political prisoners and enslaved workers. The arrival of Soviet POWs after 1941 and the decision to use Auschwitz as an extermination site for European Jewry necessitated an expansion of the site. In 1942 a huge annexe 3km away at Birkenau was built to handle the mass murder of Jews and others, and to house the enslaved workers involved in running the camp. Illustrating all aspects of the Nazi terror machine, from forced labour to torture, summary execution, medical experimentation and industrial-scale murder, the site is a crucial witness to history.

Reconstructed barracks at Auschwitz II-Birkenau

The killings

Between 1.1 and 1.5 million prisoners from more than 25 nations lost their lives at Auschwitz-Birkenau. The vast majority of victims were Jews, although tens of thousands of Poles, Roma and Soviet POWs died here too. Many perished as a result of slave labour, hunger, illness and torture, although the largest numbers were murdered after the construction of Birkenau and its gas chambers in 1942.

Liberated by the Red Army

Before retreating in 1944, the Nazis blew up the gas chambers, crematoria and many of Auschwitz-Birkenau's other installations but failed to fully destroy the evidence of their crimes – and thousands of survivors were in any case on hand to tell the full story of what happened here. The camp was liberated by the Red Army (including troops from Ukraine, Russia and all over the USSR) in 1945.

Auschwitz I

Auschwitz-Birkenau (www.auschwitz. org) was made a national museum in 1947 and a World Heritage Site in 1979. The number of visitors per day is limited and you are strongly advised to book a time slot online to avoid disappointment. Individual tourists to the Auschwitz site (not Birkenau) must join a guided tour unless they visit in the final 2–3 hours before closing – see the website for current arrangements.

A visit to Auschwitz begins at the **reception and information centre**. Here you can watch the chilling **introductory film** and buy a copy of the official guidebook, which shows the suggested route around both camps. Auschwitz and Auschwitz II (Birkenau) are 3km (2 miles) apart: a free shuttle bus connects the two.

'Arbeit Macht Frei'

From the reception, enter the Auschwitz camp past the former SS Guard House and through the notorious **entrance gate**, complete with the infamous motto, *Arbeit Macht Frei* (Work Makes You Free). Passing the former kitchens on your right, in front of you is **Block 4**, which contains the first main exhibition, outlining the story of the camp, as well as the creation of Zyklon B, the gas used to kill so many prisoners. In a room at the rear are the remains of more than seven tonnes of human hair, shorn from prisoners as they entered the camp

Glasses that once belonged to inmates

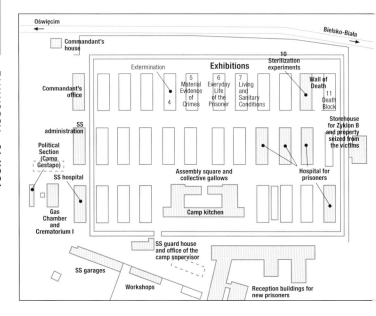

and originally intended for German clothing factories but abandoned along with the camp in January 1945.

Next door, **Block 5** displays belongings stripped from prisoners as they arrived. Most poignant are the children's shoes and toys, while the piles of glasses and artificial limbs are equally harrowing. Daily life in Auschwitz is covered in **Blocks 6 and 7**, and includes exhibitions of camp prisoner art.

Wall of Death

At the far end of the camp is the **Wall of Death**, where daily prisoners were shot for breaking the smallest of camp regulations. **Block 10** (closed to visitors) was itself an awful place: medical experiments were carried out here, mainly on female prisoners, many of whom died as a result.

Block 11 was the camp's prison, in which many of the pitch-black cells were so small that prisoners could neither sit or stand. Few survived in here. Though many of the cells were destroyed, you can visit that of Father Kolbe, a Polish priest who died here after changing places with a Jewish prisoner who survived because of

The infamous motto that greeted prisoners upon arrival

him. It was in the cellars of Block 11 that the Nazis carried out their first experiments with Zyklon B, in 1941.

National Memorials

From Block 11, turn right and you'll pass various blocks given over to **National Memorials**. These were designed by historical experts from many of the countries whose citizens died here, and are enormously valuable in documenting the Jewish and Roma communities uprooted from their homelands and sent here to be murdered.

Gas chamber

After walking through **Roll Call Square**, where – until the camp's population became unmanageable – roll call would be held three times a day, continue to the end of the row of blocks to a reconstruction of the **gas chamber and crematoria**. The gas chamber functioned from 1941–3, and was used to put to death those prisoners who were no longer fit for work. After the creation of the extermination camp at **Auschwitz II-Birkenau** in 1942, the gas chamber at Auschwitz was dismantled and the building used as an air-raid shelter by the SS.

The **gallows** in front of the gas chamber was used to hang camp commandant Rudolf Höss in 1947.

Auschwitz II-Birkenau

Whether you walk or take the shuttle bus to Birkenau you will enter via the **Gates of Hell**, one of the few parts of the camp left intact. Featured in a number of films that have been set in the camp – including *Schindler's List* – they are now almost as infamous as the *Arbeit Macht Frei* gates in Auschwitz I. Follow the original railway tracks through gates to the site of the unloading ramp, where the trains carrying Jews from all over Europe would arrive, and where selection would take place: those fit for work would be sent for processing; those declared unfit would immediately be sent to the camp's gas chambers.

In terms of camp remains, there is very little to see at Birkenau. It is a place of reflection and remembrance. Most visitors choose to walk the length of the unloading ramp to the remains of the gas chamber and crematoria, where there is a simple memorial to the victims. Two reconstructed women's barracks show the appalling conditions inmates had to endure.

From the gas chamber, walk to the 'sauna' (another reconstruction) where those chosen for work were disinfected before being assigned to barracks rife with disease. From here, walk past the Ash Pond – one of many pits where the ashes of prisoners were dumped – and trace the outline of the camp back to the Gates of Hell: its scale is terrifying. Even more so is the knowledge that it was to be extended. The vast area behind the Ash Pond was known as Mexico; it was intended for expansion.

The Gates of Hell

TOUR 16
Wieliczka Salt Mine

Explore a centuries-old subterranean world as you venture down into Poland's oldest working salt mine. Listed as a UNESCO World Heritage Site in 1978, the mine now incorporates museums, galleries, chapels, burial grounds and even an underground restaurant.

DISTANCE: (Mine tour) 3.5km (2.5 miles)

TIME: A half day

POINTS TO NOTE: Wieliczka is 10km (6 miles) from Kraków. Easiest way to get to Wieliczka is by train from Kraków's main station. Regarding tours of the mine, if you have a fear of confined spaces, this is probably not an expedition for you. It's possible to leave the tour at only a few locations, and even if you do get out early, you may need to wait your turn for the cramped cage lift to get you back up to ground level. Remember the mine is at a constant 15°C (59°F), so dress accordingly; layers are sensible. Wear sturdy shoes, too, as there are lots of steps to climb.

The town of Wieliczka, which received its charter in 1289, developed around the lucrative salt-mining trade. The salt was initially obtained from springs that bubbled up in the area, a process that was so successful that, by the fourteenth and fifteenth centuries, this had become one of the continent's most important mining towns.

Visiting the mine
Wieliczka Salt Mine (Kopalnia Soli Wieliczka; ul. Daniłowicza 10; www.wieliczka-saltmine.com; by guided tour only, available in different languages) has a 3.5km (2 mile) tourist trail that plunges to level three, some 135m (443ft) underground. It makes for a moderately strenuous two-hour tour. The descent into the mine is by stairway, although lift access can be arranged. The more physically demanding Miner's Route lasts three hours. Ticketholders are given specific time slots, and advance internet bookings are advised.

Sanatorium
Since the mid-nineteenth century, when salt baths were first recognised for their healing potential, Wieliczka has also been a **sanatorium**. Today, its underground chambers are still used for the treatment of

There are many kilometres of tunnels in the mine

respiratory illnesses, particularly asthma, and allergies. Working, too, as a modern-day health resort, visitors can book both overnight stays and day treatments. Tours of the treatment centre are available.

Level one

After being sorted into language groups in the reception area (this can involve a wait of up to an hour if you have not pre-booked), you walk down the 378 steps of the **Daniłowicz Shaft**, sunk in 1635, to level one. The shaft itself continues to level six, at a depth of 243m (800ft). At the bottom, you will be cramped into a tiny space for five minutes while the guide presents some basic information about the mine. From here you are led to the **Copernicus Chamber**, a huge room dedicated to the astronomer Copernicus, who is thought to have visited the mine in the fifteenth century while a student

at the Jagiellonian University. Next, you pass through the Baroque **St Anthony's Chapel**, which hosted its first service in 1698: it is the oldest of the mine's chapels. Almost all of the chapel's decorations and sculptures are made of salt.

There are more salt sculptures in the **Janowice Chamber** next door, while the **Burnt Chamber** is a chilling reminder of the dangers of salt mining: an explosion here in the nineteenth century killed a number of miners. The tight **Sielec Chamber** is next. Here, you can see tools used by salt miners over the centuries.

Moving to the other side of the mine, the enormous, impressive **Casimir the Great Chamber** displays an original horse-powered harness used to haul salt from lower levels, yet is merely a taster of what comes next: the **Pieskowa Skała Chamber**, one of the largest in the mine, which links level one with level two, 65m (213ft) below. Be warned: the stairs are very steep in places.

Level two

In the **Kunegunda Traverse**, you can see the original wooden drains as well as waxworks of miners hauling salt through the tunnels.

The **Holy Cross Chapel** features a Baroque wooden crucifix dating from the seventeenth century, after which you will visit the cathedral-like **St Kinga's Chapel**, probably the

Sculpture of Casimir the Great

Altar in St Kinga's Chapel

most impressive of the mine's places of worship. It features a number of bas-reliefs, all carved in salt by miners and depicting scenes from the New Testament, as well as a pulpit (also in salt) in the approximate shape of Wawel Hill. The chapel is renowned for its incredible acoustics.

From the chapel you are led downhill towards the **Erazm Barącz Chamber**, filled with one of the mine's salt lakes. The water here is 9m (30ft) deep. As you walk around the precarious wooden gallery you will wonder how on earth it was built. Continuing downhill, through the **Michałowice** and **Drozdowice Chambers**, you arrive at the deep **Weimar Chamber**, excavated in the early twentieth century and named after the Prince of Weimar who visited with the German writer and poet J.W. von Goethe in the seventeenth century.

It features some impressive salt sculptures in the various recesses and a deep brine lake at the bottom; note that the staircase that hugs the walls as you descend to level three is extremely steep.

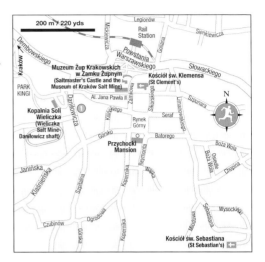

Level three

A monument commemorating Józef Piłsudski (founder of the Polish Legion during World War I and credited with restoring independence to Poland in 1918), carved in rock salt by the miner sculptor Stanisław Anioł in 1997, dominates the upper part of the **Piłsudski Chamber**. One of the first parts of the mine to be opened up as a tourist trail (by the Austrians in the 1830s), it leads past the Poniatowski Traverse to the 36m (118ft) -high **Staszic Chamber**, dedicated to Stanisław Staszic, a nineteenth-century geologist whose bust (in salt, of course) is at the top of the chamber. From here, a glass lift whisks you down to the floor of the chamber.

The surreal Kunegunda Gallery

Coming into the Wisła Chamber you will find access to facilities and the chance for a rest, and maybe view a temporary exhibition. The first part of the tour ends here in **Witold Budryk Chamber**, today a restaurant, **Karczma Górnicza**, see ①. At this point you are 125m (410ft) below the surface. There is an opportunity to buy souvenirs here, too. Beyond here is the wooden altar of **St John's Chapel**, where private masses and occasional weddings are held.

If you wish to leave the tour at this stage, you follow the signs and are whizzed back up to the top by lift. If you continue to the Kraków Saltworks Museum – run by a different company but included in your ticket– you'll visit a further sixteen chambers full of artefacts, mining equipment and miners' clothing, as well as works of art, including paintings by the Polish artist Jan Matejko. There is also a chamber displaying the most beautiful salt crystals.

Saltmaster's Castle

While you are exploring Wieliczka, it is also well worth discovering the neighbouring **Saltmaster's Castle** (Muzeum Żup Krakowskich w Zamku Żupnym; www.muzeum.wieliczka.pl). As you leave the mine, the grounds are directly opposite. Originally a thirteenth-century fortress that was turned into a Renaissance castle in the

> ### Food and drink
>
> **①** **Karczma Górnicza**
> The underground *Miners' Tavern* could be one of Europe's great tourist traps, but thankfully the mine's management have kept it simple and inexpensive. The briny atmosphere stimulates the appetite, so prepare to tuck into huge portions of Polish food, such as *żurek* (rye soup) with sausage or bigos. There is also a children's menu.

sixteenth century, this is the country's sole example of medieval architecture relating to salt mining and trading. To see an exhibition focusing on the ancient and early medieval history of Wieliczka and its surroundings, you have to go underground once more – it's in the original thirteenth- to fifteenth-century cellars.

The sixteenth-century Gothic hall, with a vaulted ceiling supported by a single pillar, is hung with portraits of the castle's former salt lords. A collection of salt cellars reflects various styles from the eighteenth to the twentieth centuries. The display also features Polish and other European porcelain.

Other buildings within the complex include a fourteenth-century Gothic bastion and defensive walls, a warehouse, guardhouse and kitchen.

St John's Chapel   Souvenir lights from the mine

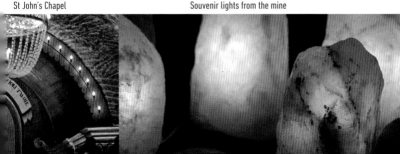

DIRECTORY

Our edit of the best hotels, restaurants and evening
entertainment to suit all tastes and budgets, plus an
A–Z of all the essential information you need to know,
a quick language guide, and some great book and film
recommendations to give you a flavour of the city.

Accommodation

At one time, Kraków's accommodation was characterised by shabby remnants of Poland's Communist past and its state-run lodgings ruled with iron-fist discipline. This once-dormant hotel scene exploded into life with the boom of the budget flight, and today visitors find themselves spoilt for choice. Expect everything from mega-brand chains to boutique hotels, family-run guesthouses to B&Bs, self-catering apartments to some of Europe's best hostels.

Accommodation will likely be your biggest expense in Kraków. While rooms are most expensive in high season, Kraków's emergence in recent times as a year-round destination means that prices stay fairly stable throughout the year. A lack of business travellers means that few hotels lower their rates at weekends either. Almost all hotels of note include breakfast in the price, with a few charging extra and the absolute minority offering no breakfast at all.

Booking in advance is advisable year-round, and essential during the high season, which kicks off around the start of June and finishes towards the end of September. If you want to stay in Zakopane, which receives fifty times its population in tourists annually, it's even more vital to book

> ### Price categories
>
> Each accommodation reviewed in this Guide is accompanied by a price category, based on the cost of a standard double room in high season. Price ranges include breakfast, unless stated otherwise.
> €€€€ = over 600zł (£120)
> €€€ = 425–600zł (£85–£120)
> €€ = 250–425zł (£50–£85)
> € = under 250zł (under £50)

in the high seasons of summer (June–Sept) or winter (Christmas–Mar).

Around Main Market Square
Elektor
Ul. Szpitalna 28; www.hotelelektor.com
A Kraków legend, where the draw of the enormous double rooms with separate lounge area has proven to be irresistible for any number of high-rolling visitors. Simply furnished, the rooms are not perhaps as luxurious as they once were, but they offer excellent value for money, and the suites especially are almost always reserved months in advance. €€€

La Fontaine
Ul. Sławkowska 1; www.bblafontaine.com
Provided you've got a strong pair of legs to conquer the stairwell, *La Fontaine* is a highly credible self-catering option.

A bed at the *Grand Hotel*

Rooms are decorated in red shades, and while the decor can't be considered snappy, you get a highly central location in return for your money. €€

Globtroter Guesthouse
Pl. Szczepański 7/15;
www.globtroter-krakow.com
Simply furnished en-suite rooms in a rickety old building with wooden staircases and verandas. In a wonderfully central spot, the hotel opens onto a walled garden that's remarkably secluded for the location and exceedingly restful. It's a bit basic and there's no breakfast – but with plenty of cafés within easy reach that shouldn't be a problem. €

Grand Hotel
Ul. Sławkowska 5–7; www.grand.pl
A stone's throw from Main Market Square, the *Grand* is a showcase of neo-Baroque interior design. Every room and suite is individually decorated and all have great bathrooms, wi-fi and discreetly positioned TVs. If you can stretch your wallet, go for one of the six suites: the Louis XVIth-style Fireplace Suite is a favourite. The hotel has the *Grand Café* and the *Grand Signature*, the latter a showcase restaurant of elegant Secessionist style, with a stained-glass dome and ornate galleries. Staff are more than happy to help translate menus that feature Polish specialities such as sole Walewska, trout and perch dishes alongside modern European favourites. €€€€

Great Polonia Kraków
Ul. Mikołajska 20; www.oldkrakow.greatpolonia.pl
Formerly known as the *Amadeus*, this grand abode has a lustrous roll call of guests, from King Charles III to the Russian dancer Mikhail Baryshnikov. Expect sublime service, large rooms full of rich furniture, and fine common areas. And it all comes at reasonable – if hardly cheap – prices. €€€€

Gródek
Ul. Na Gródku 4; www.hotelgrodek.com
During construction of the *Gródek* in 2005, an important medieval archaeological site was unearthed next door, and was immediately incorporated into the plans as a museum. It is such attention to detail – no request is too big – that sets the *Gródek* apart; that and the award-winning interior design: a modern take on old Kraków with a bohemian twist. A highlight of any visit to Kraków is a trip to the hotel's exquisite restaurant, which offers opulent surroundings and new flavours and twists on classic Polish cooking. €€€€

Hostel Rynek 7
Rynek Główny 7; www.hostelrynek7.hotelsofkrakow.com
Making super-central lodging accessible to all pockets, this clean, friendly venue has windows opening onto the Cloth Hall. With the exception of a couple of doubles, rooms follow the stack-a-backpacker mentality,

Neo-Baroque interior at the *Grand Hotel*

Room at *Hotel Pod Różą*

with wood-framed bunks squeezed into long narrow rooms. €

Leo Aparthotel
Sławkowska 4/7; www.leoaparthotel.com
Leo offers modern, well-furnished rooms and suites in the centre of Kraków. All rooms are en suite (some have been fitted with whirlpools) and some also have kitchenettes and balconies. There is no on-site restaurant. €€

Pałac Bonerowski
Ul. św. Jana 1; www.palacbonerowski.pl
One of the most historic buildings in Kraków, which in the seventeenth century served as both home and official headquarters of King Jan Sobieski, has been carefully converted into one of

the city's best hotels. There are eight simple but elegantly furnished rooms and six exquisite suites, and if their size is not immediately impressive, the decor and extras, such as the views of the Main Market Square, marble bathrooms and what they claim is 'Europe's longest chandelier', are. €€€€

Pod Różą
Ul. Floriańska 14; www.podroza.hotel.com.pl
This elegant, centrally located hotel is Kraków's oldest. With a core building dating from the Renaissance, it has some impressive period features such as the mid-nineteenth-century Neoclassical entrance, and every corner is filled with antiques. It certainly has an enviable pedigree: Tsar Alexander II of Russia, Balzac and Liszt count among the former guests. Fully renovated in 2020, the introduction of modern comforts has done nothing to diminish its historic atmosphere. The main atrium-style dining room of the restaurant tricks you into thinking you are sitting beneath a Roman sky, while the smaller *Szef Room*, where haute-cuisine tasting menus are served, caters for those seeking a more intimate ambiance. An extensive wine list is another bonus. €€€

Senacki
Ul. Grodzka 51; www.hotelsenacki.pl
Positioned halfway between the Main Market Square and Wawel, the *Senacki* has twenty traditionally decorated

The rooftop bar at *Stary*

rooms with modern bathrooms, mostly with strong showers, a few with baths. The beamed ceiling and carved stone pillars in the ground-floor dining room nod to the fourteenth-century heritage of the building, while the café-bar reveals its thirteenth-century origins. The young, friendly staff are knowledgeable and very helpful. €€€€

Stary
Ul. Szczepańska 5; www.stary.hotel.com.pl

In a building that was, for more than a century, the home of wealthy Kraków industrialists, this gorgeous pile has been renovated into a sublime hotel that seamlessly combines the medieval with the modern. So, while the rooms are wooden-floored and retain their character – including original frescoes in some cases – the bathrooms are contemporary, all with whirlpools and marble tiling. Some rooms have small balconies with views over the Main Market Square. There's also a swimming pool in the cellar and a rooftop bar. €€€€

Wentzl
Rynek Główny 19; www.wentzl.pl

The Wentzl not only has views of the Main Market Square – it is right on it. Its rich colours and personal decor create an authentic home from home. Staff are friendly and speak a number of languages. The service – as well as the location – makes up for the somewhat small and slightly

overpriced rooms. The hotel has two upmarket restaurants, on the first floor and in the cellar, plus a ground-floor café that serves what locals insist is the best ice cream in the city. €€€€

Wit Stwosz
Ul. Mikołajska 28; www.hotelws.pl

A couple of minutes' walk from Main Market Square, this historic sixteenth-century building recently been renovated in traditional style. For what you are paying, it's a bargain, offering huge, comfortable beds and large windows that flood the rooms with light. An atmospheric cellar restaurant serves great Polish and international food. €€€

Around Wawel Hill
Benefis
Ul. Barska 2; www.hotelbenefis.pl

While the onus at this three-star hotel is on functionality, the rooms are very smart, sharp and brightened with whimsical touches such as leaf-patterned duvets and dashes of modern art. €€

Copernicus
Ul. Kanonicza 16; www.copernicus.hotel.com.pl

Hiding behind a deceptive Renaissance facade is a small modern hotel, with a pool and atrium courtyard, a short walk from Wawel Hill. The rooms may not all have whirlpools, but all are equally regal in their decor: woodcarvings and marble abound amid rich wallpaper and deep carpets. Service

A sumptuous room at the *Stary*

carries a personal touch. The hotel's (expensive) upmarket restaurant offers perhaps the most adventurous Polish food in the land, and has an extensive wine list to match. There is also a spa featuring a small swimming pool, sauna and beauty treatments. €€€€

Novotel Kraków Centrum
Ul. Kościuszki 5; www.all.accor.com
Despite being part of a chain, this gem is a sound option for its array of free extras. It has a huge pool, the restaurants are excellent, and the rooms are comfortable and cosy, even if rather corporate. From the upper floors there are great views of Wawel – at no extra cost. €€

Qubus Kraków
Ul. Nadwiślańska 6; www.qubushotel.com
If the ultra-modern design isn't quite to your taste, then the views from the top-floor swimming pool over the old centre of Kraków certainly will be. Rooms are all well furnished, have lovely bathrooms, and the TVs must be among the biggest in the city. Good service and a reasonable rate make this a good choice for bargain hunters. The hotel has a trendy, split-level piano bar which is a wonder of contemporary design and has a fine cocktail list. €€

Radisson Blu Hotel Kraków
Ul. Straszewskiego 17;
www.radissonblu.com/hotel-krakow
Swedish-owned and -operated luxury, where the guest rooms – decorated in soothing pastel shades – are spacious, and the service is as fussy or as discreet as you want it to be. Bathrooms are a particular treat, with their heated floors, wide range of complimentary cosmetics and butter-soft robes. There is an on-site sauna, good restaurants and a comfortable lobby bar. Surprisingly affordable rates for the high standard. €€€

Sheraton Grand Kraków
Ul. Powiśle 7h; www.marriott.com
Well placed on the banks of the Vistula for both the Old Town and Wawel Castle, the *Sheraton Grand Kraków* is a city institution. There's a swimming pool, fine guest rooms and a clutch of restaurants and bars. The *Someplace Else* bar, with its screen showing sports, is one of the most popular expat hangouts in the whole of Poland; it's also, perhaps surprisingly, a fun place to take the children. Meanwhile, *Anima*, the *Sheraton*'s classier dining option, is a sublime mix of modern service and traditional Mediterranean cuisine. How they manage to get fish and seafood this fresh so far from the ocean is anyone's guess, but it might explain the high prices. €€€€

Kazimierz

Aparthotel Spatz
Ul. Miodowa 11; www.spatz.pl
A stylish, minimalist hotel that makes use of cream and chocolate colours. Highly recommended,

A more traditional room

though at this price you may expect a greater range of facilities. €€

Great Polonia Kraków Kazimierz
Ul. Józefa 24; www.krakow.greatpolonia.pl
A spotless three-star jaunt decorated with a fuchsia facade and rooms in pink and brown. While the rather neutral design won't stir you to flights of fancy, the welcome at the front desk is warm and the location bang in the centre of Kazimierz. €€

Eden
Ul. Ciemna 15; www.hoteleden.pl
A carefully restored fifteenth-century building now opened as a hotel, in the heart of Kazimierz. It is aimed mainly at Jewish visitors with what we are led to believe is the only *mikvah* (Jewish ritual bath) in the country. There is a sauna, a health-giving salt cave and a delightful garden, too. Good value for money. €€

Ester
Ul. Szeroka 20; www.hotel-ester.krakow.pl
In the heart of Kazimierz, opposite the Old Synagogue, and within walking distance of Wawel Castle, the *Ester*'s small scale (only fifty guests fit in when full) lends a personal touch, and staff are friendly. Rooms are well decorated in pleasant colours, and the smart, contemporary-style restaurant serves Polish and Jewish cuisine. The hotel also has parking spaces and a cellar bar. €€

The swimming pool at *Novotel Kraków Centrum*

Karmel
Ul. Kupa 15; www.karmel.com.pl
Lugging your luggage upstairs isn't much fun, and the rooms are something of a squash, but negatives aside, the *Karmel* is a treasure, with well-appointed quarters, pearly white designs and a side-street location on one of the area's quieter thoroughfares. €€€

Kazimierz's Secret
Ul. Józefa 34; www.kazimierzs-secret.com
Ten-plus apartments, all to a high standard. With names including Bishop's Apartment and Lucky Number 13, the digs are nowhere near as imaginative as you might envisage, but they still offer good-quality comfort as well as everything

Some hotels' facilities include salt rooms for 'natural healing'

from washing machines to kitchens. A good option for families. €€

Klezmer-Hois
Ul. Szeroka 6; www.klezmer.pl
Located on the principal street of the Kazimierz district, near the Tempel and Remuh synagogues, this fin-de-siècle townhouse hotel has a popular café and restaurant with live music. The ten rooms and apartments are large and clean, if a little basic (not all bathrooms are en suite), and they represent decent value for the price. €€

Metropolitan
Ul. Berka Joselewicza 19;
www.metropolitanboutiquehotel.pl
This gorgeous, upmarket boutique hotel in an elegant renovated nineteenth-century building is one of the best places to stay in the city. Rooms are tastefully decorated in contemporary style, the restaurant is top-notch (with excellent buffet breakfasts), the bar is super-cool, the gym is swanky and the service exceptional. €€€€

Regent
Ul. Bożego Ciała 19; www.hotelregent.pl
In the heart of the Kazimierz district, this historic hotel offers 39 simply furnished rooms for a great price. All rooms have en-suite facilities. The restaurant, located in the basement, is only open in the mornings to serve the excellent buffet breakfasts. €€

Room at the *Metropolitan*

Around Planty

Andels
Ul. Pawia 3; www.wyndhamhotels.com
This modern hotel situated opposite the railway station is as lovely inside as it is ugly from the exterior. Interior design is the main draw here. The powerful reds, Cubist furniture and modern technology in the rooms plus competitive room rates ensure this place is an ideal business as well as tourist choice. €€€

Ascot
Ul. Radziwiłłowska 3; www.ascotpremium.pl
Equidistant from the station and the Main Market Square, this modern hotel offers standard rooms at a nevertheless decent price. The doubles are a little small, though the triples and family

Rustic Polish interior

rooms are very well sized. All have good bathrooms, air conditioning and a super-fast internet connection. Common areas are a bit dull, but the staff are helpfulness personified. €€

Europejski
Ul. Lubicz 5 (enter from ul. Radziwiłłowska); www.he.pl
A few minutes' walk from the Planty gardens and Juliusz Słowacki Theatre, this period building offers flexible accommodation, including an attractive 'mansion-block apartment suite' at around the price of a double in a town-centre hotel. There is a stylish bar, a good restaurant and parking. €€

Fortuna
Ul. Czapskich 5; www.fortuna-hotel.hotel-krakow.net
This newly renovated period building in a neighbourhood of eclectic late nineteenth-century architecture contains a great little hotel with relatively cosy rooms and a nicely furnished restaurant/café. It also offers parking. €€

Greg & Tom Hostel
Ul. Pawia 12/7; www.greg-and-tom-home-hotelsofkrakow.net
Stags and hens are banned at this branch of the *Greg & Tom Hostel* empire, so it's odds on for a solid night's sleep. There's a friendly atmosphere here, with a multitude of facilities on offer including dinner, board games, tea and coffee.

City tours are also bookable through the hostel along with other themed trips. €

Hotel Pollera
Ul. Szpitalna 30; www.pollera.pl
Behind its classical facade, this hotel – situated opposite the Juliusz Słowacki Theatre and Holy Cross Church – shelters delightful Secessionist interiors, including a superb floral stained-glass window on the staircase. Rooms are well sized and have antique furniture and original wooden flooring. Some bathrooms have showers only (no tubs). €€

Hotel Pugetów
Ul. Starowiślna 15a; www.donimirski.com
A romantic atmosphere is harboured in this restored mansion house. Rooms are traditionally decorated with portraits of damsels adorning the walls. Fluffy bathrobes and locally sourced toiletries are provided. While lacking in lifts, *Hotel Pugetów* redeems itself with oodles of character and obliging staff. €€€

Ostoya Palace
U. Piłsudskiego 24; www.ostoyapalace.hotelsofkrakow.com
This very pretty hotel a few minutes' walk from the Main Market Square has been stylishly converted from a late nineteenth-century palace. The ambience is light and romantic, with parquet floors and traditional tiled stoves. Note that most rooms have

showers rather than baths. The cellar bar is a cosy cave to retreat into in bad weather. Some may find it a drawback that the restaurant is only open for breakfast and not in the evenings. €€

Polonia
Ul. Basztowa 25; www.hotel-polonia.com.pl

Opened in 1917, this elegant Neoclassical hotel is right by a main traffic junction, but the thick double glazing ensures a peaceful night's sleep in all of the comfortable – if spartan – rooms. Great location for sightseeing opposite the Planty Gardens, and near the railway station. There's a charmingly old-fashioned restaurant serving Polish staples. €€

Polski Pod Białym Orłem
Ul. Pijarska 17; www.donimirski.com

This classical building next to the Czartoryski Museum and Florian's Gate, overlooking the original city walls, conceals a very comfortable hotel. Standard rooms are rather on the small side but traditionally furnished with good bathrooms. The deluxe rooms and suites are well worth the extra, if you can afford it. Rooms and common areas are decorated with fine tapestries and reproductions of classic works of Polish art. €€€

The Secret Garden Hostel
Ul. Skawińska 7; www.thesecretgardenhostel. hotelsofkrakow.com

A wonderful hostel in a city packed with hostels. This colourful place has comfortable dorm-style rooms, as well as simple, immaculately clean private doubles, triples and quad rooms. Add in use of a washing machine, lockers and luggage storage, and you have the perfect backpacker stopover. And yes, it has a secret garden. €

Wielopole
Ul. Wielopole 3; www.wielopole.pl

Another bargain bolthole midway between the Old Town and Kazimierz, the *Wielopole* stands out for the polished attitude of the staff that can never do enough for you. The guest rooms are stylish, with simple showers, cable television and free internet in every room. €€

Kraków outskirts
Farmona Spa Hotel
Ul. Jugowicka 10c; www.hotelfarmona.pl

A short drive south of the centre, the *Farmona Spa Hotel* is something of a tranquil oasis away from the bustle of the city. Surrounded by parkland, it has room for up to sixty guests, who can enjoy the hotel's range of wellness and beauty treatments, which all use natural skincare products. The rooms and suites are decorated in modern, albeit slightly dated, style, but they offer very good value for money, given the price. The hotel's restaurant, the *Magnifica*, is a good addition to the Kraków dining scene; book in advance if you want to bag a table on the balcony during summer. €€

A twin room in traditional style

Zakopane
Aries Hotel and Spa
Ul. Zaruskiego 5; www.hotelaries.pl

This luxury hotel in the centre of Zakopane boasts stylish, ornately carved wooden accents in the lavish interior. The *Halka* restaurant serves a vast buffet breakfast, great coffee and delicious dinners. There is also a bar and indoor pool and spa area as well as stunning views of the mountains. €€€€

Crocus
Ul. Chałubińskiego 40; www.hotelcrocus.pl

A lovely modern hotel close to the Wielka Krokiew ski jump. *Crocus* has large comfortable rooms and apartments available as well as a small luxury wooden house which can accommodate six to eight people. Facilities include a spa, an indoor pool and the *Vernus* restaurant. €€

Gospoda Pod Niebem
Ul. Droga Stanisława Zubka 5; www.podniebem.pk

A charming wooden house on top of Gubałówka Hill. Expect little in the way of extras but prepare yourself for the invigorating smell of pine, more fresh air than you could ever wish for, a folksy on-site restaurant and a fantastic view of the Tatras. For the price and location, you can't really find any place better to stay. €

Grand Hotel Stamary
Ul. Kościuszki 19; www.stamary.pl

For the extra expense of staying here you get large rooms, decorated in fin-

Grand Hotel Stamary

de-siècle style yet all featuring the latest in modern conveniences. Service is exemplary from immaculately attired staff. Only the location (next to the resort's grotty bus station) lets it down a little, but once you're inside the hotel, you won't mind. €€€€

Sabała
Ul. Krupówki 11; www.sabala.zakopane.pl

A giant chalet planted on Zakopane's busiest street, rooms come with log-cutter furnishings and warming winter extras such as heated bathroom flooring, while the sauna and pool are among the best in town. Noise from the live mountain bands that lurk the streets can be a problem. €€€

Restaurants

Eating out is one of the pleasures of visiting Kraków. There is a wealth of good restaurants in the city, and almost all have outside seating during the summer. While Polish cooking itself is tasty and filling enough to keep anyone happy for a short trip, the cosmopolitan nature of Kraków means that there is also a vast range of restaurants serving a variety of cuisines from all over the world. Particularly impressive are the Italian and sushi sectors. Even vegetarians – neglected in other parts of Eastern Europe – will have plenty to choose from (although watch out for the ubiquitous pork fat).

Not, surprisingly, the Old Town features the best choice of restaurants in the city, from stalls selling spicy lamb and falafel delicacies to ostentatious tourist traps with Western prices. It's the best place to try traditional fare in fairytale surroundings. Waiting staff in all but the most basic of city-centre restaurants speak English.

Be careful when paying in a Kraków restaurant: saying 'thank you' when you hand over money to a waiter or waitress signifies that you do not require any change. Also note many of Kraków's restaurants close surprisingly early, and most take their last kitchen orders some time before the published closing time. Arriving

Eating out price codes

Each restaurant and café reviewed in this Guide is accompanied by a price category, based on the cost of a two-course meal (or similar) for two, including a bottle of wine.
€€€€ = over 200zł (over £40)
€€€ = 125–200zł (£25–£40)
€€ = 70–125zł (£15–£25)
€ = under 70zł (under £15)

at any restaurant much after 10pm will usually warrant shakes of the head and the words 'Kitchen's closed'.

Old Town

Ambasada śledzia
Ul. Stolarska 8/10; tel. 662 569 460
Something of a temple to traditional Polish bar food, the "*Herring Embassy*" is a cross between a late-night pub and a stand-up buffet, serving fried herring, marinated ribs, pork knuckle and other staples. A "Polish tapas" menu features tasty portions of cabbage, pickled gherkins and bread smeared with lard. Shots of vodka and other beverages are cheap, making this a popular late-night stop-off. €

Balaton
Ul. Grodzka 37; www.balaton.krakow.pl
Stuffed peppers and fiery goulashes are the mainstay of this veteran restaurant,

Traditional Polish street food

which deserves particular praise in a city that prefers to pander to the timid Polish palate. In a certain light *Balaton* can appear tired and shabby, but that changes when the sun sets, and Roma bands stroll between the candlelit tables. €€

Bonjour Pho
Ul. Krupnicza 12
Only a short hop across the Planty from the Old Town, this cosy Vietnamese bistro is an excellent source of inexpensive eats. Pho soups come in beef, chicken and vegan variations, there's a sizzling selection of wok-fried dishes, and some delicately spiced curries. The set lunches (Mon–Fri till 4pm) are great value. €

Café Camelot
Ul. św. Tomasza 17; tel: 012 421 01 23
On a quiet corner a few steps from the city's main square, this busy ground-floor café serves light meals, excellent salads and is famed for its apple cake. €€

La Campana
Ul. Kanonicza 7; www.lacampana.pl
This uthentic, top-quality Italian restaurant, housed in the lovely House Under Three Crowns, serves good pastas and risottos, as well as fish and meat dishes. There is a pleasant garden for summer dining. €€€

Cyklop
Ul. Mikołajska 16; tel: 012 421 66 03
A friendly place with simple decor, *Cyklop* serves the best pizza in the

city, which is cooked in a traditional, wood-fired oven. It is deservedly popular, so expect to queue during peak hours or even share a table; no advance reservations. €€

Cyrano de Bergerac
Ul. Sławkowska 26;
www.cyranodebergerac.com.pl
A regular and proud winner of the *Best Restaurant in Galicia (Lesser Poland)* award. This achievement might not sound like a big deal in a region not known for the quality of its dining establishments, but *Cyrano de Bergerac* would be a contender whatever the locale or standard of competition. This is opulent dining in the extreme, with prices to match. The fillet steak is excellent, as are the Polish highlights, such as *pierogi* (Polish dumplings filled with anything from minced pork or beef to cabbage and potato or sweet berries). A superb list of French wines befits the superior cellar setting of high ceilings and antique furniture. There is also a delightful courtyard garden for alfresco dining in the warmer summer months. €€€€

Hawełka
Rynek Główny 34 (ground floor);
www.hawelka.pl
Still the first choice for those looking for a formal dining venue, this place long ago lost its crown as the city's best eatery. That said, the food remains very good – if a tad expensive – and the service as

Polish pizzas

stuffy and fussy as you would expect. For a splurge it takes some beating. €€€

Indus Tandoor
Ul. Sławkowska 13–15; www.indus.pl

Photographs of India's most sumptuous palaces line the walls of one of Kraków's finest Indian restaurants. Poles have yet to really take to Indian food, so expect a solely foreign clientele, and dishes that will not be as hot as you might normally expect. Ask the waiter nicely, however, and they will ask the chef to spice things up for you. €€€

Kawaleria
Ul. Gołębia 4; www.kawaleria.com.pl

This is a special night out: the cooking wins awards and the surroundings and service are dashing. The menu is Polish with a modern slant, changing with the seasons, and often features wild boar or venison. There's a romantic garden for summer dining. €€€€

L Concept 13
Rynek Główny 13; tel: 012 617 02 12

This is one of the more upmarket cafés on the square, yet remains a good place to unwind while sightseeing around the Old Town. Coffee, tea, cocktails, cakes, sandwiches and gourmet nibbles all served at relatively expensive prices. €€€€

Metrum Restobistro
Ul. Świętego Tomasza 43; tel: 661 322 370

This unpretentious sixth-floor lunch spot comes with a rooftop terrace and stunning views of the Old Town skyline. Offering simple and hearty dishes (including at least one vegetarian choice) at bargain prices is *Metrum*'s main selling point, with set two-course menus changing every day. There's also a rather tempting chiller cabinet full of cakes and puddings. €

Miód i Wino
Ul. Sławkowska 32; www.miodiwino.pl

A good choice to fill hungry faces amid suits of armour and stuffed animal heads, this medieval-feel favourite comes complete with waiting staff in traditional costumes and an extensive menu to leave all but the most ravenous feeling satisfied. Try the classic *żurek* soup, a national classic made from fermented rye flour. €€€

Miód Malina
Ul. Grodzka 40; www.miodmalina.pl

With one of the most welcoming hearths in Poland, this lovely little restaurant is packed out most nights, so book ahead. The food is good, based on the cuisine of Małopolska (Lesser Poland), with plenty of game. €€€

Nowa Prowincja
Ul. Bracka 3; tel: 012 430 59 59

A cute café famed for its good coffee, excellent hot chocolate and bookish clientele, *Nowa Prowincja* is also well worth considering for a quick lunch. Toasted sandwiches, hummus platters and slices of quiche are guaranteed to

Tempting fare

keep the wolf from the door; while the apple and lemon meringue pies provide reason enough to drop by. €

Padre
Ul. Wiślna 11; www.epadre.pl
Padre has a charming terrace during the summer and a gorgeous, unpretentious cellar restaurant for the colder months. The menu is slanted towards Polish and Mediterranean cuisines, with some highly tempting desserts. The wait staff are pleasant enough, and the piped music is always entertaining. €€€

Pierogarnia domowa
Ul. Szpitalna 3; tel: 695 300 712
Just off the Small Market Square this busy little place is dedicated to *pierogi*, the crescent-shape pastry parcels that play such an important part in Polish cuisine. As well as ubiquitous varieties stuffed with minced meat or cottage cheese, there are a few unusual variations – beetroot and goats' cheese being one tangy favourite. Sweet versions with strawberry or apple make for an unusual, if slightly stodgy, dessert. €

Pod Gruszką
Szczepańska 1; www.restauracjapodgruszka.pl
Elegant decor and attentive staff mark out this traditional restaurant just off the Main Market Square. Signature Polish fare such as duck, trout and *gołąbki* (stuffed cabbage leaves) are here presented with haute-cuisine finesse.

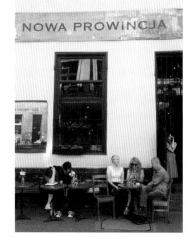

Nowa Prowincja

With a luxuriant cheesecake, it's a good idea to leave room for dessert. €€€€

Przypiecek
Ul. Sławkowska 32; www.przypiecek.pl
Dedicated to the art of *pierogi*, *Przypiecek* serves a seemingly endless variety of stuffings, with lentil and buckwheat-filled versions well worth sampling. Order and pay at the counter, then pick up your food from the hatch. If you don't like disposable plates, this is not the place for you. €

Smak Ukraiński
Ul. Grodzka 21; tel: 012 421 92 94
Something of a Kraków institution although it has changed location more

Szara's dining room

than once, "*Taste of Ukraine*" is pretty much what you might expect from the title: food and drink from Poland's eastern neighbour, served up in folksy welcoming surroundings. Staples include Ukrainian *borscht*, filled dumplings and stuffed cabbage leaves. The *okroshka* cold soup with cucumber, chicken and cream makes for a refreshing summer lunch. €€

Szalone Widelce
Ul. Szpitalna 40; www.szalonewidelce.pl

This mostly-Polish-with-a-hint-of-Italian restaurant is a hearty eaters' favourite, with pork chops, ribs, skewer-kebabs and other meaty meals served on wooden platters. There's a solid range of soups, and the weekday lunch menus are a steal. €€

Szara
Rynek Główny 6 (corner ul. Sienna); www.szara.pl

Understated, discreet but excellent, *Szara* is now a mainstay of the Main Market Square, and an essential part of a trip to Kraków. Don't panic if you can't bag an outside table: inside is a treat, with beautifully painted vaulted ceilings and large tables only adding to the joy of dining here. The food lives up to its surroundings, with delicious dishes like goats' cheese in honey and Provençale rabbit. €€€€

Szara Gęś
Rynek Główny 17; www.szarages.pl

For beautifully presented Modern Polish cuisine beneath ancient vaulted

ceilings you can't do much better than the "*Grey Goose*". Duck, lamb, fish and the (perhaps inevitable) roast goose dominate the main-course menu, although you should leave room for the signature dessert, an egg-shaped confection of mousse, chocolate and cream. €€€€

Taco Mexicano
Poselska 20; www.tacomexicano.pl

The stone cellar interior of this taco and tapas bar is a nice enough place to eat, and the food is surprisingly good. This is a spicy and refreshing change from the Polish/European restaurants that otherwise have a monopoly on the Old Town. The nachos are tasty, though the portions are small, and the main courses are better value: try the quesadillas with prawns. €€€

Trattoria Soprano
Ul. św. Anny 7; www.trattoriasoprano.pl

Kraków is full of substandard Italian restaurants; this is an exception. You will find good, simple Italian food, such as *papardelle* with salmon and mascarpone, at reasonable prices. The setting is pleasant: a spacious room decorated in Mediterranean shades. €€

U Babci Maliny
Ul. Sławkowska 17; www.kuchniaubabcimaliny.pl

In keeping with its name ("*At Your Granny Malina's*"), this eatery (hidden away towards the back of an unpromising academic building) serves up dishes

The traditional *U Babci Maliny*

typically cooked by a Polish granny. It's all great value and so popular that another branch has opened in Kraków at ul. Szpitalna 38. Classic peasant food – fermented rye soup with potatoes and sausage, *grochówka z grzankami* (pea soup with croutons), *placki ziemniaczane* (grated potato pancakes) – is served in generous quantities. It's self-service: order at the counter and pick up a number, which flashes on a small screen when your meal is ready. €

Wentzl
Rynek Główny 19; www.restauracjawentzl.com.pl
A Kraków legend, with a restaurant pedigree going back to 1792, *Wentzl* offers a classic Polish menu that is extended by Viennese specialities. Given its imposing pavement facade and the ground-floor café's icing-sugar colour scheme, the 'fine-dining' restaurant rooms in the cellar and on the first floor are something of a surprise, as is the quality of the fresh foie gras. The decor is best described as a meeting of vaulted antiquity with postmodern metalwork sculptures. €€€€

Wesele
Rynek Główny; www.weselerestauracja.pl
Even in a square lauded for its restaurants, *Wesele* stands out as something special. Rustic interiors feature plenty of flowers and carpentry, while the food scores highly for fantastic translations of local dishes. The goose is a highlight, although those wishing

to sample it might want to book a table ahead. The roe deer marinated in red wine, goes down a treat, too. €€€€

Wierzynek
Rynek Główny 15; www.wierzynek.pl
Older than any other restaurant in the city, this place can trace its history back to a banquet served here in 1364. It occupies two Renaissance houses, and there is a selection of elegant, antique-furnished dining rooms where quality Polish dishes are served. *Wierzynek's* own-brand chocolates make for a unique sweet-tooth souvenir. €€€€

Kazimierz
Ariel
Ul. Szeroka 18; www.ariel-krakow.pl
Choose from pavement tables, a sheltered courtyard with a goldfish pond, or the conservative, 1970s-style dining room with paintings depicting Jewish life. There's plenty of choice on the Polish/Jewish menu, with classics such as herring fillets in sour cream, fried *kreplah* and carp sautéed with onions and mushrooms. The second-floor room has live music nightly. A small bookshop in the entrance hall sells guidebooks and souvenirs from Kazimierz. €€€€

Barka Alrina
Bulwar Kurlandzki (at the top of ul. Gazowa, near the Kładka Bernatka footbridge); tel: 668 820 454
It's difficult to surprise the cool hipsters of Kazimierz, but this restaurant has

Polish pastries

generated a lot of praise. Located on a Dutch barge, there is dining on deck in the warmer summer months and a smart modern interior with a separate bar area for less fine days. The seasonal menu offers traditional Polish ingredients, including sheep's cheese, venison and berries, prepared in a modern way. There is also a simple children's menu for younger diners. €€€€

Dawno Temu na Kazimierzu
Ul. Szeroka 1; www.en.szeroka1.com

This terrific little restaurant is disguised to look like a row of early twentieth-century traders' shops and is topped with awnings relating to Kazimierz's Jewish past. Inside, it is a riot of antiques – all bought or found in the area – with an enjoyable clutter that is hard to dislike. The food is pretty standard Jewish fare; though note that the restaurant is not kosher. €€€

Fabryka Pizzy
Ul. Józefa 34; www.fabrykapizzy.pl

Kazimerz's *Pizza Factory* has been a trusted source of authentic thin-crust pies for many a year, serving up inexpensive fare in minimalist but homely surroundings. The (mostly traditional Italian) pizzas are generous in size and come with reassuringly stringy mozzarella cheese. It's not just about pizzas either; the choice of pasta dishes and soups of the day are perfect for lunches. Popular, so expect to queue. €€

Keladi
Ul. Józefa 5; tel: 698 331 919

A smart but welcoming Malay-Indonesian restaurant serving up a tantalising selection of medium-spicy noodle and rice dishes, including an exemplary slow-cooked chicken rendang. Look out, too, for the own-recipe drinks you're unlikely to find elsewhere in Kraków city centre, including the bandung rose syrup made with condensed milk. €€

Marchewka z Groszkiem
ul. Mostowa 2 7; www.marchewkazgroszkiem.pl

An appealingly homely restaurant with wooden floors and antique furniture, "*Carrots and Peas*" serves traditional Polish fare prepared with a touch of culinary panache and invention. Roast meats and duck feature heavily on the list of main courses, with *kluski* (Silesian dumplings) the frequent accompaniment. *Placki* (grated potato pancakes) are something of a house speciality, and here come with a multitude of toppings. The *cepelinai*, zeppelin-shaped potato dumplings stuffed with minced meat, are reliable stomach-fillers. €€

Momo
Ul. Dietla 49; tel: 609 685 775

Famous throughout Poland, this small and assuming wholefood and vegetarian restaurant between the Old Town and Kazimierz provides good healthy food, from brown rice dishes to a range of

Historic Wierzynek

excellent salads. Don't be put off by the canteen appearance – there are some truly appetising dishes whipped up in the kitchen here, representing excellent value for money. Cash only, no cards; come prepared. €

Nolio
Ul. Krakowska 27

An upmarket but youthful Italian restaurant with chic clubby decor, *Nolio* offers some of the most imaginative pasta in the city, with dishes like lamb *rotolo*, seafood *pappardelle* and duck *cappelletti* (a bit like tortellini) featuring on an exciting and regularly updated menu. Pizzas form a large part of what *Nolio* is about, with traditional recipes based on Italian-sourced, controlled-origin ingredients. There's plenty in the way of soups, salads and bruschetta if you want something light and quick for lunch. Be sure to reserve a table in advance at weekends. €€€

Polakowski
Ul. Miodowa 39; www.polakowski.com.pl

Grab a tray, join the queue, then scoop out freshly prepared meat and vegetables from steaming-hot containers before settling down with low-cost diners eating the local way. Operating since 1899, the *bigos* here is as legendary as the venue itself. Distinguishing *Polakowski* from the classic milk-bar experience are an English-language menu, rustic countryside decorations and a toilet that flushes. €

Somnium Bar
Ul. Meiselsa 5; tel: 570 063 888

This pleasant minimalist café has the added bonus of a good summer terrace. Ideal for a morning coffee or afternoon tea with a hearty piece of mouthwatering cheesecake. A wide selection of simple yet tasty dishes are also available. €€

Zalewajka
Ul. Wąska 2; www.zalewajka.com

Combining tradition with modernity, *Zalewajka*'s (the name of a Polish soup) chef serves Polish fare with a twist to hungry patrons. Apart from the eponymous *zalewajka*, expect all the Polish specialities including *pierogi* (Polish dumplings), *golonka* (pork cooked in beer) and *placki ziemniaczane* (grated potato pancakes) for prices that won't ruin your budget. €€

Kraków outskirts
Willa Decjusza
Ul. 28 Lipca 17a; www.vd-restauracja.pl

It's a bit of a trek to reach this eatery from the centre of town, and it is off the scale price-wise, but it's certainly worth the effort and expense to dine on well-prepared Italian, Polish and other European dishes within the palatial Italianate Renaissance *Willa Decjusza* (*Villa Decius*); the grand restored building is a feast in itself. Finely attired waiters make you feel very special as they whisk away huge silver domes to reveal beautifully crafted food. Only open to pre-booked groups in winter.

The wonderfully named *Dawno Temu na Kazimierzu* (*Once Upon a Time in Kazimierz*)

Nightlife

Should you feel like dancing, taking in a music concert or going to the theatre, Kraków can oblige.

Theatre and cabaret

Juliusz Słowacki Theatre
pl. Świętego Ducha 1; www.teatrwkrakowie.pl
Grand edifice staging Polish and foreign classic and contemporary drama.

Narodowy Stary Teatr
Ul. Jagiellońska 1; www.stary.pl
Though performances are usually in Polish, there are times during the year when local cultural centres sponsor performances in other languages.

Music

Harris Piano Jazz Bar
Rynek Główny 28; www.harris.krakow.pl
An archetypal cool jazz bar that does great drinks at very reasonable prices.

Jazz Club u Muniaka
Ul. Floriańska 3; www.jazzumuniaka.club
One of Kraków's most legendary jazz clubs at the bottom of a flight of stairs in a fourteenth-century cellar. Great acoustics and an intimate atmosphere.

Opera Krakowska
Ul. Lubicz 48; www.opera.krakow.pl
The Opera Krakowska has existed since the late nineteenth century, but lacked its own performance space until 2008 when it moved into a 720-seat building with outstanding acoustics.

Piwnica pod Baranami
Rynek Główny 27; tel: 012 422 01 77
Home to the Kraków Jazz Festival, this former old palace is the best place in town to watch cabaret and listen to jazz.

Szymanowski Philharmonic
Ul. Zwierzyniecka 1; www.filharmoniakrakow.pl
You can enjoy Szymanowski Philharmonic performances most nights of the week, with matinée concerts on Sundays.

Bars and clubs

Alchemia
Ul. Estery 5; www.alchemia.com.pl
A true bastion of Kazimierz cool, this venue has been attracting playwrights and artists since its inception in 1999. Scruffy antiques and faded photographs often go unnoticed thanks to the near-Stygian blackness.

Baccarat
Ul. Stolarska 13; www.baccaratclub.pl
Kraków's swankiest dance den is dripping with chandeliers and glittery trimmings. The ruthless door policy rewards the decadent.

Baroque
Ul. św. Jana 16; www.baroque.com.pl
Small and dark, this luxurious-looking restaurant-bar wins prizes

Getting the party started

for a cool atmosphere. Serves some of the best drinks in the city centre, including a whopping selection of over a hundred vodkas, adds a local flavour to your evening.

Bracka 4
ul. Bracka 4; www.klub.krakow.pl/b4
Rated by many as one of the best clubs in town, *Bracka 4* specialises in house, R'n'B and old-school music. Some of the city's best DJs play here along with live music performances.

CK Browar
Ul. Podwale 6/7; http://ckbrowar.pl
Kraków's microbrewery attracts every social type, from track-suited teens to foreign beer enthusiasts, with a roomy cellar location and sports broadcasts.

Eszeweria
Ul. Józefa 9
A famously laidback drinking den in Kazimierz, *Eszeweria* comes across as an appealing jumble of styles, with an antique-peppered interior that looks like your great-grandmother's parlour and a shaggy jungle of a garden out the back.

Movida
Ul. Mikołajska 9; www.movida-bar.pl
A long, narrow space plastered with candid pictures of celebrity patrons practising their best pouts, *Movida* is one of the classiest places in town with cocktails that blow the competition sideways.

Piękny Pies
plac Wolnica 9; www.ckbrowar.pl
A Kraków legend that has changed locations several times, "*The Beautiful Dog*" functions as both bar and club and attracts arty bohemians and dedicated drinkers. There's more musical variety here, with indie, reggae and other genres muscling in on the usual dancefloor hits.

Space Club
ul. Szewska 4; www.spaceclub.tv
This bright, big, brash, laser-illuminated club just off the man square attracts a hedonistic crowd pretty much every night of the week. With more than one floor, it offers up a choice between mainstream disco fare or more discerning grooves.

Cinema
Kino Pod Baranami
Rynek Główny 27; www.kinopodbaranami.pl
A traditional cinema rather than a multiplex, in a main-square courtyard with an art-house repertoire and bags of atmosphere.

Cinema City
Ul. Podgórska 34; www.cinema-city.pl
Modern multiplex inside Galeria Kazimierz shopping mall. Screens big Hollywood films.

Cinema City IMAX
ul. Zakopiańska 62; www.cinema-city.pl
One of the biggest screens in Poland, this is the place to come for the ultimate IMAX experience.

Intimate jazz club

Essentials

Accessible travel

All new buildings and building renovation work in Poland must meet rigid EU standards concerning the provision of accessible facilities. Places in Kraków such as the airport, many hotels and quite a few restaurants are now up to good European standards, despite the difficulty of reconciling the preservation of the UNESCO-listed heritage of a medieval city with the needs of wheelchair-users.

Kraków's cobbled streets and many of its best sights remain hard work for wheelchair-users and travellers with limited mobility. Most hotels only have a modest handful of accessible rooms so book well in advance to be sure of a place.

Many buses and trams have been adapted for wheelchair users. Electronic departure boards at each stop inform passengers of the next approaching wheelchair-accessible service.

Galeria Stańczyk (ul. Królewska 94; tel: 012 636 85 84) is a cultural centre for disabled visitors.

Addresses

In Poland, the street name is written first, followed by the house or building number. Streets are usually numbered odd on one side, even on the other, though in many parts of Old Kraków, rather more arbitrary systems are used.

Business hours

Banks open early, usually at 8am, and stay open until about 6pm. All banks are closed at weekends. During the week, shops open at 9am or 10am and stay open until about 7pm, with shorter hours on Saturdays; many are closed on Sundays. Exceptions include shops inside big shopping malls, and markets; the latter are open by 5am and generally stay open until the middle of the afternoon. Museums and galleries generally open at 10am, and close any time from 2pm to 6pm. Most museums are closed on Mondays.

Climate

Winters are crisp and snowy, with December and January typically cold, damp and foggy. However, Kraków looks magnificent in the snow, and the surrounding attractions, such as Zakopane, Poland's premier ski resort, are in full swing. Summers are usually hot and sunny from May to September, though September and October can be very wet. During the winter a warm coat, hat and gloves are required; even during the summer a light raincoat is advised.

Wawel Cathedral

Crime and safety

Although Kraków is generally safe, all cities pose a potential threat, so take sensible precautions. Don't leave coats hanging around with valuables in the pockets, or leave your mobile phone on a table. Take care when travelling on busy trams and in any crowded space, especially outdoor concerts. As in any city of this size, exercise caution when walking around late at night. Stick to well-lit streets, and if in doubt, use a taxi. Areas to be avoided late at night include the main railway station, the Planty gardens and ul. Westerplatte.

Customs regulations

Since Poland joined the EU in 2004, duty-free allowances no longer apply to travellers arriving from or leaving for other EU countries. However, some EU countries have imposed their own limits on what can be imported from Poland.

Dogs and cats may be brought into the country, providing they are microchipped or tattooed, have a pet passport and certificates for the correct vaccinations from a vet who should check current regulations with the Polish embassy in your own country.

Most Polish antiques and artworks that are not registered and not more than fifty years old can be freely exported. If permission is needed, you can apply at the Wojewódzki Urząd Ochrony Zabytków (ul. Kanonicza 24; necessary forms at www.wuoz. malopolska.pl) but a good antique dealer will take care of the paperwork for you. This can take a few months and may involve extra taxes.

Electricity

Electricity is 220v AC, 50 Hz. Sockets are round with two-pins. Those from the UK, US and outside Continental Europe need an adaptor. US and non-European visitors whose countries use a 110v system need a voltage converter, though they are not necessary for most mobile phone and laptop chargers.

Embassies and consulates

Consulates (in Kraków)
US: ul. Stolarska 9; tel: 012 424 51 00; www.pl.usembassy.gov/ embassy-consulate/krakow.

Embassies (in Warsaw)
Australia: ul. Nowogrodzka 11; tel: 022 521 34 44; www.poland.embassy.gov.au.
Canada: ul. Matejki 1/5; tel: 022 584 31 00; www.international. gc.ca/poland-pologne.
New Zealand: al. Ujazdowskie 51; tel: 022 521 05 00; www.mfat.govt.nz/en/ countries-and-regions/europe/poland.
Republic of Ireland: ul. Mysia 5; tel: 022 564 22 00; www.ireland.ie/en/poland/warsaw.

Horse-drawn carriage on Market Square

All dressed up for Easter

South Africa: ul. Koszykowa 54; tel: 022 622 10 05; https://dirco1. azurewebsites.net/warsaw.
UK: ul. Kawalerii 12; tel: 022 311 00 00; www.gov.uk/world/poland.

Emergency numbers

In an emergency, call 999 for an ambulance, 997 for police, 985 for mountain rescue or 998 for the fire brigade. You can also call 112 for all general emergencies. **SOS for foreigners:** tel: 800 200 300 – receive advice from English-speaking consultants.

Health

EU nationals: EU citizens with a valid European Health Insurance Card (EHIC) or UK citizens with a Global Health Insurance Card (GHIC; available from UK post offices or online at www.services. nhsbsa.nhs.uk/cra/start) can receive free emergency treatment, although private medical insurance is recommended. State healthcare in Poland is underfunded and poor. Bear in mind that salaries for state medical staff are low, and that 'gifts' are common and often necessary.
North Americans: You will need to take out medical insurance before travelling. While emergency treatment is technically free, all other services must be paid for.

Centrum Medicover (tel: 500 900 500; www.medicover.pl) operates a network of medical centres in Poland's major cities, including Kraków. It has English-speaking staff, a broad range of specialists and an ambulance service. Its programme includes home visits, and it will treat non-members. Medical services are also provided by Falck (tel: 022 535 91 00; www.falck.pl) and Scanmed (tel: 012 629 88 00; www.scanmed.pl).
Dentists: Dentists who speak foreign languages can be booked at the private clinic Scandinavian Clinic, pl. Szczepański 3 (tel: 012 421 89 48; www.scandinavian-clinic.pl), and Dentamed, ul. Na Zjeździe 13 (tel: 012 259 80 00; www.denta-med.com.pl).
Pharmacies: There are several pharmacies (Apteka) offering a 24hr service throughout the city, including those at ul. Galla 26 and ul. Karmelicka 23. For more information on all-night pharmacies, see www.krakow.pl/nasze_miasto/ 145442,artykul,apteki.html.
Water: The local tap water is safe to drink.

Internet

There is a surviving handful of inexpensive internet cafés in the centre, such as the 24hr *Hetmańska* (ul. Wiślna 4), but they are fast becoming redundant, as practically every café and restaurant offers wi-fi to customers. Look out, too, for the hotspot Cracovia logo signalling free wi-fi at hotels and cafés.

Several pharmacies in Kraków offer a 24hr service

LGBTQ+ travellers

Catholic Poland is a largely conservative country, with a far-from-enlightened attitude to members of its LGBTQ+ community. That said, Kraków's city authorities have in recent years been more open to the LGBTQ+ community than those in the rest of the country. In the 2011 parliamentary elections, the liberal Palikot Movement's Anna Grodzka polled a large number of votes and became Europe's first transgendered MP.

The age of consent for homosexuals, as well as heterosexuals, is 15. Handy gay information to the city can be found at www.travelgay.com/?s=krakow.

Maps

Free city maps can be picked up in tourist information centres, hotels, bars, restaurants and cafés. A good map of Kraków is Compass's 1:50,000 scale edition, which covers the city in detail, lists public transport routes and has the only decent map of Nowa Huta in print.

Media

Newspapers: Polish broadsheets include *Dziennik Polski* (*Polish Daily*) and *Gazeta Wyborcza* (*The Electorate's Newspaper*). The official listings website, *Karnet Kraków* (www.karnet.krakow.pl), has events information in English and publishes a bimonthly paper magazine *Kraków Culture*

with interesting features. *Kraków In Your Pocket* (www.inyourpocket.com/poland/krakow; bimonthly) is an entertaining alternative, available from newsagent kiosks, hotels and Empik outlets, as is the English-language monthly newspaper *Kraków Post* (www.krakowpost.com), which is good for local news.

Television: Most hotels have satellite TV offering English-language stations such as CNN and BBC World.

Radio: Local radio stations include Radio Kraków (www.radiokrakow.pl) on 101.6 FM, and Jazz Radio 101 FM. Polskie Radio's Polish news in English (www.thenews.pl) is available as a podcast or smartphone app.

Money

Currency: Poland's currency comprises złoty (paper notes and coins) and groszy (coins): 100 groszy equal 1 złoty. Groszy coins come in denominations of 1, 2, 5, 10, 20 and 50. Smaller denominations of złoty (1, 2 and 5 złoty) are coins; higher denominations (10, 20, 50, 100 and 200 złoty) are in the form of paper notes.

Bureaux de change: The best place to change money is in a bank, and there are many in the city centre, all offering similar exchange rates. While exchange kiosks and counters (marked Kantor) throughout the city offer better rates, they also apply large commission charges. Beware

For news, the *Kraków Post* is an English-language monthly newspaper

signs declaring 'No Commission': these usually apply only when Polish currency is being sold.

Cash machines: Cash machines (ATMs) are the easiest way to get local currency. You'll find them spread throughout central Kraków.

Credit cards: Internationally established credit cards, including American Express, Visa and MasterCard, are accepted by numerous hotels, restaurants and shops. Don't expect smaller establishments to accept credit cards, particularly not for small sums.

Cash advances on credit cards can be arranged at a number of banks, including Bank Pekao SA, Rynek Główny 31. Bring your passport.

Post

Post offices: The post office near the main railway and bus stations, at ul. Lubicz 4, offers a round-the-clock daily postal service for stamps, letters, money transfers and fax. The post office at ul. Westerplatte 20 is open Mon–Fri 8am–8pm, Sat 8am–2pm, but closed on Sun.

Stamps for postcards and letters abroad cost 10zł to destinations in Europe, 12zł to North America. Red post boxes have a logo of a yellow post horn in a blue oval.

Public holidays

1 January New Year's Day
6 January Epiphany
March/April Easter Sunday and Easter Monday
1 May Labour Day
3 May Constitution Day
May/June Pentecost (7th Sunday after Easter)
June Corpus Christi (9th Thursday after Easter)
15 August Feast of the Assumption
1 November All Saints' Day
11 November Independence Day
25 December Christmas Day
26 December St Stephen's Day

Religion

Most Poles are Roman Catholic. Mass is said in English at 10.30am on Sundays at Kościół św. Idziego (St Giles, on ul. Grodzka towards Wawel).

Though less common, Kraków also has churches and houses of worship for other denominations and faiths. These include Kościół św. Marcina (Church of St Martin, Lutheran Congregation) on ul. Grodzka 58, Kościół Chrześcijan Baptystów (Baptist church) on ul. Wyspiańskiego 4 and the Methodist Church on ul. Długa 3. Kazimierz's Remuh Synagogue (on ul. Szeroka 40) is the only synagogue where Friday services are held regularly. To participate, contact the Jewish community centre in advance (tel: 012 370 57 75).

Telephones

Phone numbers: To call Kraków from outside the country, dial your

St Joseph's opulent interior

international access code followed by 48 for Poland and the subscriber number minus the initial 0.

If you're calling a Kraków landline from anywhere in Poland, dial the 10-digit number beginning with 012. The same applies for calling a landline from a Polish mobile with the exception of Plus GSM, which requires the dropping of the first 0.

To get a line out of Poland, dial 00 plus whatever you need after that for the country in question (Australia 61, UK 44, US and Canada 1).

For directory enquiries in English when in Kraków, telephone 118 811.

Mobile phones: Citizens of EU and European Economic Area (EEA) countries do not pay temporary roaming charges in Poland. UK operators have different policies on roaming in the EU (some offer free data roaming, others are more complicated) and you should check your contract before leaving home.

Visitors from other countries can avoid roaming costs by using a local prepaid SIM card. Several companies now offer extremely cheap start-up packages for less than 10zł, with top-up cards costing 5zł and upwards. Both can be bought from shops and kiosks around the city as well as the airport, and bus and railway stations.

Time zones

Polish time is one hour ahead of GMT.

Kraków smiles

It's customary to tip restaurant staff

Tipping

It is customary to tip restaurant staff, taxi drivers and hotel porters about 10–15 percent.

Note that when paying in a restaurant, if you say 'thank you' when handing over the money the waiter will assume that he may keep the change. To make sure you get your change back say '*proszę*' as you hand over the money.

Toilets

Kraków has been working on improving the public toilets in the city. There are now several with disabled access such as where ul. św. Tomasza meets the Planty. But,

Town Hall Tower clock

whether it's a public convenience, or in a café or restaurant, vigilant attendants often demand that you pay – usually 1zł or 2zł (although this habit is gradually dying out).

Women's toilets are marked with a circle, men's with a triangle.

Tour operators

Kirker Holidays (www.kirkerholidays.com) offers short breaks to Kraków, while Baltic Holidays (www.balticholidays.com) offers packages as well as tailor-made trips, as does Regent Holidays (www.regent-holidays.co.uk), a long-time specialist in Eastern Europe.

Tourist information

In Kraków

The official **Kraków City Tourist Office** has several InfoKraków (www.infokrakow.pl) branches throughout the city:
Cloth Hall, Main Market Square 1–3
Wyspiański Pavillion, pl. Wszystkich Świętych 2
ul. Szpitalna 25
ul. św. Jana 2
ul. Józefa 7, Kazimierz
ul. Zgody 7, Nowa Huta
Other information centres include:
The Jewish Cultural Information Office (Centrum Kultury Żydowskiej, ul. Meiselsa 17, Kazimierz; www.judaica.pl) has information on Jewish cultural events.

Zakopane Tourist Information Centre (www.zakopane.pl) sells good hiking maps as well as a decent guide to the resort's ski-run network and lift-ticket system.

Outside of Poland

UK: Polish National Tourist Office, 10 Heathfield Terrace, London W4 4JE; www.poland.travel.
US: Polish National Tourist Office, 5 Marine View Plaza, Hoboken, New Jersey, NJ 07030; www.poland.travel.

Transport

Arrival

By air: Kraków's John Paul II International Airport at Balice is the second-busiest airport in Poland, served by direct flights to and from many European cities throughout the year. Flight time from London is just over two hours. Seasonal direct flights operate from cities such as Chicago and New York.
By rail: There are various train routes between London and Kraków, involving as many as six or as few as two changes. One of the quickest involves changing in Paris and then Berlin and takes a little less than 24 hours; though the route via Brussels, Cologne and Frankfurt is faster it involves more changes. Deutsche Bahn (www.bahn.com) books train journeys across Europe.

Postcards for sale

There are also regular train services between Kraków and other main Polish cities. Express trains between Kraków and Warsaw, which need to be booked in advance, take about 2hr 45min. For information and booking contact Polish State Railways (Polskie Koleje Państwowe; www.pkp.pl).

Neither PKP telephone lines nor train station information desks have many English speakers, though staff will try to find someone to help you, but the colour-coded timetables are easy to follow: yellow for departures (*odjazdy*); white for arrivals (*przyjazdy*).

Express trains usually feature the prefix 'ex', and direct trains are indicated as *pospieszny*. Trains marked *osobowy* are slow, sometimes very slow.

The main railway station is within easy walking distance of the historic centre, though the traffic system obliges taxis leaving the terminus to take a slightly more circuitous route to the centre.

By road: Coach travel is very cheap in Poland. In Kraków, regional and international coaches leave from the coach station (Małopolski Dworzec Autobusowy; www.mda.malopolska.pl) in ul. Bosacka 18 next to the railway station. The journey from Kraków to Warsaw can be long because coaches often stop at a number of cities en route.

Airport
Kraków's John Paul II International Airport (ul. Kapitana Medweckiego 1; www.krakowairport.pl) is located 18km (11 miles) east of the city in Balice.
Getting to the city: The best option is by train (single ticket Kraków airport – Kraków Główny: 17zł, Kraków airport – Wieliczka Market Square: 21zł). Public buses 209 (every 30min) and 300 (1 hourly) both make the journey and there is also a night bus 902 (single ticket for all buses 6zł); turn right out of the international terminal to find the bus stop. Alternatively, outside the terminal you'll find plenty of official Kraków Airport Taxi (tel: 012 258 02 58) waiting. The fare to the city centre ranges from 69zł to 89zł depending on location.

Transport within Kraków
Public transport in Kraków is both cheap and reliable. The fabulous tram system provides the perfect way of getting around, from 5am to 11pm. Tram tickets cost 4zł for a 20min ride (sufficient for most trips in the town centre) or 6zł for a single trip of up to 60min. Better value are 24hr (17zł), 48hr (35zł) and 72hr (50zł) tickets. A family weekend ticket (25zł) allows unlimited travel for 1–2 adults and up to five kids on Saturdays and Sundays. Buy them from

InfoKraków centres dot the city

Buses are cheap and reliable

most kiosks, or anywhere you see a 'Sprzedaż biletów MPK' sign.

Tickets must be validated in one of the yellow machines when boarding. Watch a local do it first if you're unsure.

Be careful when getting off trams in the city centre, where they share the roads with cars: you're essentially stepping down into traffic, and drivers do not always give tram passengers priority.

For bus and tram information, see www.mpk.krakow.pl.

Trains: The newly modernised main railway station, just a short walk from the historic centre, is Kraków Główny (Dworzec Główny, pl. Jeziorańskiego 3, tel: 703 200 200).

You can catch a train from here to Oświęcim for the Auschwitz-Birkenau concentration camp and to the Wieliczka salt mine.

Taxis: Although the town centre is essentially pedestrianised, taxis do have access. There are cab ranks around Main Market Square, although it is not very practical or necessary to use taxis to get around the centre. Radio taxis, which can be booked by phone, are generally cheaper than taxis from ranks, though the latter are not very expensive.

For longer journeys, negotiate the fare with the driver before departure. Some reliable cab companies are:
Mega Taxi, tel: 012 196 25; www.megatazi.eu
Radio Taxi, tel: 012 191 91; www.radiotaxi919.pl
Radio Taxi Wawel, tel: 012 196 66; www.waweltaxi.pl

Expect to pay a 7zł starting rate plus 2.50–7zł per kilometre depending on time of day.

Uber is present in Kraków although its drivers don't have access to the pedestrianized town centre.

Car rental: Kraków's compact size generally makes hiring a car more trouble than it's worth. However, for visiting other destinations, a car can be a good idea.

Arrangements and conditions for car hire are similar to those in other countries. The minimum age requirement is 21 and you must have been in possession of a valid licence for at least one year. US and Canadian licences are accepted, as are international driving licences. Ask if collision damage waiver insurance is included in the price.
Avis: ul. Lubicz 23; www.avis.pl (also at the airport)
Budget: ul. Lubicz 23; www.budget.pl
Krakrent: ul. Kamieńskiego 41; www.krakrent.pl
Europcar: Kraków airport; www.europcar.com.pl
Hertz: al. Focha 1 (inside the Cracovia Hotel); www.hertz.com.pl

A good train network connects Kraków with surrounding attractions

Joka: ul. Rakowicka 10b;
www.joka.com.pl
National: ul. Medweckiego 1
(airport); www.nationalcar.com
Driving: It's a sobering fact that
Polish traffic fatality figures are
among the worst in Europe, a
testament to the appalling condition
of the roads and the often-unsafe
driving practices of the locals.

For those who insist on driving in
Kraków, be warned that roadworks
are everywhere. If you find yourself
following a tram on a stretch of
road that doesn't have a separate,
fenced-off area for them, proceed
with caution. You are expected to
stop when trams do, regardless of
what lane you're in, as people will be
getting on and off, and will be doing
so via the road you are driving down.

You can drive in Poland on an EU
or US licence. Dipped headlights
must be switched on at all times year-
round; seat belts are compulsory
front and back and the maximum
blood-alcohol limit is 0.02 percent.

Poles drive on the right-
hand side of the road.

Speed limits are 140kmh (87mph)
on motorways, 120kmh (75mph) on
dual carriageways, 100kmh (62mph)
on single carriageways, 90kmh
(56mph) outside urban areas, and
50kmh (31mph) in built-up areas
during the daytime and 60kmh
(37mph) at night. You may be
fined on the spot for speeding.

Parking: Because of the frequency of
car theft and break-ins in and around
the city, it's advisable to use guarded
car parks. There are only two car
parks in the centre, at Plac św. Ducha
and Plac Szczepański. Neither is very
large, and both are very popular.

Additional car parks within
walking distance of the centre include
by the main railway and bus stations,
pl. Biskupi, ul. Zyblikiewicza, ul.
Lubicz, Galeria Krakowska, and
ul. Powiśle by Wawel Castle.
Petrol (gas): Petrol stations are
common on major roads; most stay
open around the clock and all sell the
full range of petrol, diesel and lpg.

Visas and passports

Holders of EU passports do not
need a visa to enter Poland and may
stay as long as they please. Visitors
holding passports from many other
countries may also enter Poland
without a visa, but their stay may
be limited, usually for ninety days.

Poland is a member of the
Schengen group of countries,
meaning that a Schengen Block
visa is valid for entry to Poland.

Travellers may need to fulfil
additional medical, insurance
and financial requirements to be
granted a visa. Minimum visa
processing times range from ten
days to a month, depending on the
passport held, and can take longer.
Be sure to allow plenty of time.

Kraków Główny, the newly modernised railway station

Language

Polish, a Slavic language, has a complex grammar and can be difficult to pronounce with its long sequences of consonants. As a general rule, the accent falls on the penultimate syllable. The majority of tourist industry staff in Kraków speak good English and/or German, and efforts have been made in recent years to translate signs and menus for English-speaking visitors. Attempting a few basic words is likely to be appreciated by the locals, however.

General

Yes *Tak*
No *Nie*
Please *Proszę*
Thank you *Dziękuję*
Excuse me *Przepraszam*
You're welcome *Proszę*
Hello/Hi *Dzień dobry/Cześć* **(informal)**
Goodbye *Do widzenia/
Cześć* **(informal)**
Do you speak English? *Czy
mówisz po angielsku?*
I don't understand *Nie rozumiem*
I'm sorry *Przepraszam*
I don't know *Nie wiem*
My name is... *Mam na imię...*
Nice to meet you *Miło poznać*
What is your name? *Jak masz na imię?*
I am English/American
Jestem z Anglii/z Ameryki
When? *Kiedy?*

At what time? *O której?*
today *dzisiaj*
yesterday *wczoraj*
tomorrow *jutro*
now/later *teraz/później*
morning *rano*
afternoon *popołudnie*
evening *wieczór*
day/week *dzień/tydzień*
month/year *miesiąc/rok*
left *lewo*
right *prawo*

On arrival

**Where is there a bus/tram
stop?** *Gdzie jest przystanek
autobusowy/tramwajowy?*
railway station *dworzec kolejowy*
airport *lotnisko*
cab rank *postój taksówek*
one-way ticket *bilet w jedną stronę*
return ticket *bilet w dwie strony*
I'd like a single/double room *Poproszę
pokój jednoosobowy/dwuosobowy*
**What is the charge per
night?** *Ile kosztuje doba?*

Emergencies

Help! *Pomocy!*
Call a doctor/an ambulance
Proszę wezwać lekarza/karetkę
Call the police/fire brigade *Proszę
wezwać policję/straż pożarną*
Where's the nearest hospital?
Gdzie jest najbliższy szpital?

Trilingual exit sign

I am sick *Jestem chory(a)*
I have lost my money/passport/luggage *Zgubiłem(am) pieniądze/paszport/bagaż*
pharmacy/chemists *apteka*

Shopping

How much is it? *Ile to kosztuje?*
Have you got…? *Czy ma Pani/Pan…?*
enough *wystarczy*
too much *za dużo*
a piece *kawałek*
each *każdy*
Do you take credit cards? *Czy można płacić kartą?*
Is there a bank/ATM near here? *Czy jest w pobliżu bank/bankomat?*
shopping centre (mall) *centrum handlowe*
market *rynek*
supermarket *supermarket*
open *otwarte*
closed *zamknięte*

Sightseeing

Where is…? *Gdzie jest…?*
tourist information office *informacja turystyczna*
church *kościół*
exhibition *wystawa*
museum *muzeum*
guide *przewodnik*
free *za darmo*

Dining out

breakfast *śniadanie*
lunch *lunch/obiad*
dinner *kolacja*

meal *posiłek*
first course *pierwsze danie*
main course *drugie danie*
the bill *rachunek*
I am a vegetarian *Jestem wegetarianinem/wegetarianką*
I'd like to order *Chciał(a)bym zamówić*
tip *napiwek*
smoking *dla palących*
non-smoking *dla niepalących*

Days of the week

Monday *poniedziałek*
Tuesday *wtorek*
Wednesday *środa*
Thursday *czwartek*
Friday *piątek*
Saturday *sobota*
Sunday *niedziela*

Numbers

0 *zero*
1 *jeden*
2 *dwa*
3 *trzy*
4 *cztery*
5 *pięć*
6 *sześć*
7 *siedem*
8 *osiem*
9 *dziewięć*
10 *dziesięć*
20 *dwadzieścia*
30 *trzydzieści*
40 *czterdzieści*
50 *pięćdziesiąt*
100 *sto*
1000 *tysiąc*

Hairdresser sign

Books and film

Poland has a long, proud literary tradition that stretches back to medieval times, when scribes such as Jan Długosz (1415–80) chronicled the events of the era. In the following centuries, Polish talents including the Romantic poet Adam Mickiewicz (1798–1855) and the Nobel Prize-winning author Henryk Sienkiewicz (1846–1916) came to the fore, blending Romanticism with patriotism during a time when Poland was under foreign rule. As Poland's self-declared cultural capital, Kraków was awarded UNESCO's City of Literature in 2013.

In late May/early June, the city is home to the Kraków International Film Festival, one of the most respected film festivals in Poland. The city may not be Poland's answer to Hollywood (that title goes to Łódź), but Kraków has an intriguing real and filmic history.

Books

Fiction

Solaris, by Stanisław Lem (1921–2006). Science-fiction writer and former Jagiellonian University medical student stands out as one of Poland's best-known authors, with his seminal work twice turned into film.
The Captive Mind, by Czesław Miłosz (1911–2004). Miłosz is popularly considered as Poland's finest writer of the twentieth century,

and his 1953 defining masterpiece, is a fascinating study of the human psyche. Miłosz was awarded the Nobel Prize for Literature in 1980.
The Books of Jacob, by Olga Tokarczuk (1962–). Roaming evocatively across the landscapes of Southern Poland and the Habsburg Empire, this extraordinarily rich book won the Nobel Prize for Tokarczuk in 2018.
The Madman and the Nun and **The Crazy Locomotive**, by Stanisław Ignacy Witkiewicz (1885–1939). Also known as Witkacy, he was one of the great avant-garde figures of inter-war Poland. Heavily influenced by drugs and depression, his works include plays, paintings and novels.

Holocaust

Schindler's Ark, by Thomas Keneally (b.1935). This novel, set in Schindler's Podgórze factory and the nearby Płaszów labour camp, paints a vivid picture of wartime Kraków.
If this is a Man, by Primo Levi (1919–87). Levi, an Italian chemist and Holocaust survivor, tells his story, with detached prose picking up the minutiae and describing in detail the dehumanisation process experienced by inmates.
This Way for the Gas, Ladies and Gentlemen, by Tadeusz Borowski (1922–51). Borowski describes

Ida, 2015 Academy Award winner for Foreign Language Film

his incarceration in Auschwitz. A chilling story of daily survival.
Auschwitz, by Sybille Steinbacher (b.1966). This recent book provides a fine historical overview.

Poetry
Despite penning fewer than 250 poems, Kraków-based Wisława Szymborska (1923–2012) won international recognition when awarded the Nobel Prize for Literature in 1996.

Film

Schindler's List
Based on Thomas Keneally's 1982 book ***Schindler's Ark***, Steven Spielberg's 1993 film ***Schindler's List*** tells the true story of Nazi Party member and businessman Oskar Schindler (1908–74; see page 85), who moved to Kraków shortly after the German invasion in 1939 and opened a factory in Podgórze. The factory was staffed by Jewish employees, whom Schindler did his best to protect, with the film following the story through to the final liquidation of Kraków's Jews and Schindler's mostly successful attempts to save his staff. Ralph Fiennes' portrayal of SS camp commandant Amon Göth is a tour de force.

Polish film
Man of Marble (1977). Daring Communist-era film covering the career of an award-winning shock-worker on Kraków's Nowa Huta and his fall from grace with the authorities.
The Double Life of Veronique (1991). Affecting Polish-French drama from director Krzysztof Kieślowski with scenes shot in Kraków.
The Pianist (2002). Roman Polański's Oscar-winning film of the true story of a Polish-Jewish pianist's life in World War II Warsaw, episodes of which were shot in Kraków.
Karol: A Man Who Became Pope (2005). A biography of Karol Wojtyła who was Bishop of Kraków and went on to be Pope John Paul II.
Katyń (2007). Tells the story behind the infamous Katyń Massacre in which the KGB murdered 20,000 Polish officers in 1940. Directed by long-time Kraków resident Andrzej Wajda.
Walesa. Man of Hope (2013). Another key film from Wajda, this tells the story of Nobel Peace Prize winner Lech Wałęsa and the Solidarity Movement.
Ida (2013). Paweł Pawlikowski's black-and-white drama in which a young woman discovers her past after being orphaned in World War II won the 2015 Academy Award for Foreign Language Film.
Cold War (2018). A love story of two mismatched people set in Paris, Poland, Berlin and Yugoslavia. Paweł Pawlikowski won the Best Director's award for this movie at the 2018 Cannes Film Festival.

Oskar Schindler's factory

Auschwitz features in many films

About this book

CREDITS

The Rough Guides Walks & Tours series helps you discover the world's most exciting destinations through our expert-curated trip plans: a range of walks and tours designed to suit all budgets, interests and trip lengths. These walks, driving tours and site excursions cover the destination's most quintessential attractions as well as a range of lesser-known sights, while food and drink stops for refreshments en route are highlighted in boxes. If you're not sure which walk to pick, our Best walks & tours for... feature suggests which ones work best for particular interests. The introduction provides a destination overview, while the directory supports the walks and tours with all the essential information you need, as well as our pick of where to stay while you are there and select restaurant listings, to complement the more low-key options given in the trip plans.

About the authors

Rough Guides Walks & Tours Kraków was thoroughly updated by Jonathan Bousfield, whose work builds on original content by authors Ian Wisniewski, Renata Rubnikowicz, Craig Turp, Jackie Staddon and Hilary Weston.

Help us update

We've gone to a lot of effort to ensure that this edition of the **Rough Guides Walks & Tours Kraków** is accurate and up-to-date. However, things change – places get "discovered", new gems open up, restaurants and rooms raise prices or lower standards. If you feel we've got it wrong or left something out, we'd like to know, and if you can remember the address, the website, whether or not it was free to enter – so much the better.

Please send your comments with the subject line "**Rough Guides Walks & Tours Kraków Update**" to mail@uk.roughguides.com. We'll acknowledge all contributions and send a copy of the next edition (or any other Rough Guide if you prefer) for the very best emails.

Credits

Rough Guides Walks & Tours Kraków

Editor: Joanna Reeves

Authors: Jonathan Bousfield, Craig Turp, Ian Wisniewski, Renata Rubnikowicz, Jackie Staddon, Hilary Weston

Picture Editor: Piotr Kala

Picture Manager: Tom Smyth

Cartography: Katie Bennett

Layout: Grzegorz Madejak

Head of DTP and Pre-Press: Rebeka Davies

Head of Publishing: Sarah Clark

Photo credits: Accor 109T; Corrie Wingate/Apa Publications 4BL, 4C, 4BR, 7CT, 7B, 10/11, 12L, 13R, 16/17, 20, 21, 27, 30, 31R, 32/33, 34, 34/35, 36, 36/37, 49R, 50, 50/51, 51R, 52, 52/53, 53R, 54, 55, 56, 58/59, 59R, 60/61, 62, 63R, 65R, 64/65, 67, 68, 69R, 70, 71, 73R, 74, 74/75, 75R, 77R, 78, 81R, 82, 83R, 82/83, 84, 85R, 86, 86/87, 87R, 88, 88/89, 89R, 91, 92/93, 93R, 94, 95, 96, 97, 98, 98/99, 100, 100/101, 101R, 115, 121, 125R, 126, 127, 128, 128/129, 129R, 130, 130/131, 131R, 134, 135, 137R; Dreamstime 10, 11R, 12/13, 14, 15, 26, 37R, 38/39, 62/63, 64, 79, 84/85, 112/113, 116, 124, 124/125; Franek Vetulani 117T; Grand Hotel Stamary 113T; Gregory Wrona/Apa Publications 6TC, 6BC, 7T, 7CB, 16, 18, 19R, 18/19, 40, 41, 43R, 44, 45, 46, 46/47, 47R, 48, 48/49, 57R, 56/57, 58, 61R, 66, 76/77, 80, 104, 105, 106, 107, 108, 109, 114, 117, 118, 119, 120, 122, 123; iStock 80/81, 110/111; Leonardo 106T; Mary Evans Picture Library 22; Metropolitan 110T; Shutterstock 1, 4T, 6TC, 6BC, 8/9, 17L, 23T, 23B, 24/25, 28, 29, 30/31, 32, 33R, 35R, 42, 42/43, 60, 68/69, 72, 72/73, 73T, 74T, 76, 90, 92, 99R, 102/103, 129T, 132, 133, 136, 136/137

Cover credits: Bazylika Mariacka **Sergey Dzyuba/Shutterstock**

Printed in Czech Republic

Distribution

UK, Ireland and Europe
Apa Publications (UK) Ltd
sales@roughguides.com

United States and Canada
Ingram Publisher Services
ips@ingramcontent.com

Australia and New Zealand
Booktopia
retailer@booktopia.com.au

Worldwide
Apa Publications (UK) Ltd
sales@roughguides.com

Special Sales, Content Licensing and CoPublishing

Rough Guides can be purchased in bulk quantities at discounted prices. We can create special editions, personalised jackets and corporate imprints tailored to your needs.
sales@roughguides.com
http://roughguides.com

Index

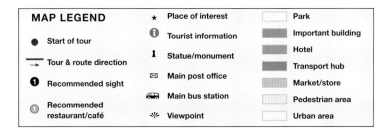

MAP LEGEND

- ● Start of tour
- → Tour & route direction
- ❶ Recommended sight
- ⓘ Recommended restaurant/café
- ★ Place of interest
- ⓘ Tourist information
- 1 Statue/monument
- ✉ Main post office
- 🚌 Main bus station
- ☀ Viewpoint
- Park
- Important building
- Hotel
- Transport hub
- Market/store
- Pedestrian area
- Urban area